Civility in America

ESSAYS FROM AMERICA'S THOUGHT LEADERS

PRESENTED BY THE DILENSCHNEIDER GROUP, INC.

in conjunction with

THE CARNEGIE COUNCIL FOR ETHICS IN INTERNATIONAL AFFAIRS

CIVILITY IN AMERICA. Copyright © 2011 DGI PRESS

Printed in the United States of America
First printing, 2011
ISBN-13: 978-0-9839007-0-2

DGI PRESS
THE DILENSCHNEIDER GROUP, INC.
200 PARK AVENUE, 26TH FLOOR
NEW YORK, NY 10166
WWW.DILENSCHNEIDER.COM

Cover design and DGI PRESS logo by Jaye Medalia
Project management/interior design by Laura E. Kelly

★

*All of civility depends on being able to contain
the rage of individuals.*

—JOSHUA LEDERBERG

CONTENTS

★

Joel H. Rosenthal

President, Carnegie Council for Ethics in
International Affairs

Civility is a core principle of public life. Without it we live in Thomas Hobbes's world where life is "solitary, poor, nasty, brutish, and short." Everyday life is indeed a struggle to fulfill our duties to self, family, and community. As we go about our daily rounds, we see that conflicts are unavoidable, limits are tested, and patience is worn away. Civility is our answer to Hobbes's idea that life is no more than a "war of all against all." Civility offers a better way to live.

Civility is based on the idea that we should take into account the interests of others. We should treat others the way that we would like to be treated ourselves. As a child growing up in Massachusetts, I learned of the story of Lake Chaubunagungamaug. Translated playfully from the Native American Nipmuc language it means, "You fish on your side, I fish on my side, and nobody fish in the middle." In addition to the funny sounding name and legends about its origin, it came to symbolize Native American, Yankee and frontier wisdom. Civility is perhaps at its most useful when it helps us find ways to work through conflicts and live amicably with differences.

Civility is about respect and accommodation. It is also about virtues and standards. We enact civil behavior by following manners and proper etiquette. We show respect by following rituals such as using appropriate language, dressing appropriately for occasions, and deferring to those more senior or to those who need assistance, depending on the circumstances. These actions routinize expectations of courtesy and make it part of our daily lives.

Civility in business, politics, the media, and everyday life does not mean that competition, dissent, and conflict should end. Rather, it means that in the midst of the tough circumstances, we remember to treat individuals with dignity and respect, and to honor the standards set by those whom we admire.

The participants in this series are worthy exemplars. As you read their thoughts on the challenge we face in maintaining high standards of civility today, remember that each has been tested by experience. They each recognize how much poorer we would be if we did not take time to reflect and reaffirm our commitment to the principle of civility, especially given the acids of modern life that threaten to dissolve it.

It has been said that everyone is talking about civility but no one is doing anything about it. Robert Dilenschneider decided to step up to the challenge. We are grateful for his idea for the original lecture series and for his sponsorship of it. As The Dilenschneider Group celebrates its 20th anniversary, we thank Bob and his firm for their commitment to such an important issue facing our country and the world.

★

Rev. Theodore M. Hesburgh, CSC

President Emeritus of
the University of Notre Dame

Given the turbulent times we are experiencing in every sector of society and recognizing the stakes that will determine the shape and future of the next generation, I can think of few civic issues that are as important as decency and civility in society.

During my 35 years as President of the University of Notre Dame, I always felt my duty was to create an environment that produced young members of society who were not only highly educated and well-prepared, but also respectful and open-minded. Through the challenges we confronted during my tenure, I sought to engender a sense of awareness and civility in my students that would allow them to be productive world citizens.

Civility was treasured and valued, although it was frequently tested during the tumultuous period of our nation's history of the 1960s and the 1970s, when the Vietnam War pitted sons against fathers, citizens against politicians and students against established society.

These were contentious times, and very often Americans confronted one another philosophically and violently on issues such as civil rights, feminism, peace and justice.

President Dwight D. Eisenhower appointed me as one of the first members of the newly formed U.S. Commission on Civil Rights during an era in modern history when Americans drank at different water fountains and sat separately on public buses based on the color of their skin. These were not times of civility. They were times of civic and spiritual turmoil.

BUILDING A HIGHER PLATFORM

America moved beyond that divisive period, despite the protests, the political assassinations, and such convulsive events such as the 1968 Democratic Convention in Chicago. Now, we urgently need to build on what we have created and move to a still higher platform. We need to recognize that incivility has again crept into our society and raised its ugly head in a way that threatens the fabric of American life. Indeed, incivility seems to have gained social acceptance at a time when we should be at relative peace, working together to move into the 21st century.

In many ways, we remain a nation divided, most especially by political rhetoric, as President Obama pointed out in his remarks at a memorial service eulogizing the six people slain in Tucson by a mad-man during an assassination attempt on U.S. Rep. Gabrielle Giffords. Our political rhetoric was intense before the shootings, and that national tragedy only seemed to escalate it, the President noted.

He wisely said, "At a time when our discourse has become so sharply polarized, at a time when we are far too eager to lay the blame for all that ails the world at the feet of those who think differently than we do, it's important for us to pause for a moment and make sure that we are talking with each other in a way that heals, not a way that wounds."

We are a nation in need of healing. During the last election, hundreds of million of dollars were spent on advertising designed to demonize political opponents. Incivility has become an accepted vice at all levels of society, and a recent poll concluded that 75 percent of Americans believe the nation has become demonstrably ruder and less civil.

Many of us are shouting at others, and even more of us are shouting just for the sake of shouting on the Internet, in newspaper columns, in political ads, on talk radio, at the stop light, at the dinner table, at the negotiating table, in the halls of high schools and in the halls of Congress.

While we are more technologically advanced than at any point in history, we are reverting back to primitive personal behavior that characterized mankind before we became "civilized."

The result is that there is strife throughout America, screaming blogs, political attacks, vicious reader comments, and the inability to work across the legislative aisle without rancor and insult.

RESTORING RESPECT

This incivility is most apparent in the media on talk radio and TV shows where callers are degraded and guests demeaned. There is no civil dialogue in any of this. Sadly, most of us have observed the same tendencies—possibly learned from watching the pundits and politicos do their thing—in our interpersonal relations.

Even in family life, incivility is apparent, and if TV sitcoms are a projection of our lives, or an inspiration for them, what we encounter is disrespect at all levels, from parent to child and child to parent. The problem at its most fundamental level is the result of a lack of respect for other people, a dehumanizing of the individual.

We somehow sense this is wrong. We were not meant to treat one another this way. We are meant to treat others as we wish to be treated. Civility is a foundation of society, of political discourse, of friendship, of social intercourse and of family life.

Consider that our society, which for the most part is more affluent than others, more educated than others and more technologically advanced than others, has somehow stumbled in its progress. Now it's time for us to get up and stand erect as human beings were meant to, and behave with dignity and integrity.

This book, which collects a series of 2011 Carnegie Council lectures sponsored by The Dilenschneider Group on the occasion of its 20th anniversary, is an attempt to restore a measure of civility in our dealings. Some of the greatest minds in the media, business and government explore this crisis and offer their insights into possible solutions.

The voices of reason they raise and the thoughts they offer make an invaluable contribution to the restoration of civility in American society.

★

Philip K. Howard

on
Civility in Society

I hope that you won't be too offended by what I say about civility and law; and, if you are, that you will be civil in your disagreement.

My interest, for the last decade and a half, has been in considering the relationship between authority and freedom. What I've concluded is that the growth of law has corroded the institutions of authority in our society, with many deleterious effects, and one of the victims of that is our sense of ethics and civility.

What I mean by "civility" is a concept that actually goes back to the origins, which is the norms and manners required to live in a city, in a crowded place, which is where the word comes from. We live in a crowded world now, which is increasingly interdependent, and we have to have norms that allow us to interact more freely.

It's not just the absence of rudeness, which is another way that we commonly think of civility. The phrase also embodies adherence to ethical codes of behavior, to basic honesty in human dealings, and, perhaps more importantly than anything else, respect for the common good. The higher the level of civility, the higher the level of trust in society in these often anonymous dealings; and the higher the level of trust, studies repeatedly show, the greater both our economic and our psychological well-being.

Talking about the norms of how we relate to each other is actually an extraordinary subject. Civility is how we define our culture. There was a wonderful scholar, judge, and cabinet minister in England about 100 years ago called Fletcher Moulton. He gave a great talk, which was then reprinted in *The Atlantic* in 1924, called "The World of Manners." He said there were three great domains of human action:

One was the domain of positive law, where law tells us what to do and we have to abide by the law in a free society.

The second was the domain of free choice, where we can do whatever we want to do and no one will think otherwise. That's what living in a free society is: we have this open field of freedom where we can act according to our instincts.

But then, he said, there is this great area in between called the world of manners, and it's this area in between, he argued, that defines a culture, and that ultimately the success of the culture depends on how we maintain this world of manners.

He put it this way: "Between 'can do' and 'may do' ought to exist the whole realm which recognizes the sway of duty, fairness, sympathy, taste, and all the other things that make life beautiful and society possible." So it's all the norms of how we relate to each other in so many ways that ultimately define our success as a culture.

Lord Moulton concluded that this was the area of society that was most important, but also most unenforceable, because it depends on people's values. I agree with that partially, but I disagree with it profoundly in another way, which I will get to at the end.

So if we look at American society today and you polled Americans and you ask "How are we doing from the standpoint of our civil norms and such?"— and there have been many recent polls addressing this—you will find that we're not doing very well.

A March 2011 Harris Poll found that 87 percent of the public believes our political system imbues society with anger and ill temper and is counterproductive to the health of our society. Eighty-seven percent in a poll is virtually unanimous.

Similar other polls in the same time found approval rating for Congress at 7 percent. That's also more or less matching numbers.

We've all seen the attack ads in every election. It swayed the last election. They attacked the other side based on arguments that were half truths, and probably more untruths, and yet they were successful in several Republican races. We don't approve of them, and yet we know it rubs off on the culture.

Many moderate observers believe that the Gabby Giffords shooting in Tucson was a result of this ill temper—almost distemper—of our political system that appears to be designed to polarize the public rather than to make legitimate arguments.

You'd have to say, when you look at the political debate, that there are almost no legitimate solutions in sight. One party essentially has as its main platform "no new taxes" and the other party has as its platform "we're not going to touch any entitlements." My friend Will Marshall, who runs the Progressive Policy Institute, commented recently that "It's not true that bipartisanship is dead in Washington—there's a perfect bipartisan conspiracy to bankrupt the country."

If you look at corporate America, you'll see a same phenomenon of self-interested action, where CEOs manage for short-term profits, not for long-term health (say, with research and development), and seem to manage for very large, oversized compensation packages—not, again, necessarily conducive to restoring trust in the society.

You go to schools. The culture of respect is nonexistent in most urban public schools. Public Agenda did a survey for us a few years ago where they found that 43 percent of the high school teachers in America say they spend more time maintaining order than they do teaching. Think about what that means. That means the students in those classes are getting, at most, half the learning that they're supposed to get.

What happened to order? That has actually been studied by Richard Arum at NYU, among others. It turns out there's a direct correlation between the rise of due process and the decline in order in America's schools.

Public Agenda also did a survey about law in schools, and found that 78 percent of the middle and high school teachers in America have been threatened with lawsuits for violations of the rights of their students by their students.

Now, it's not that they would mostly sue and if they sued they would win, but think of what it says about the corrosion of authority of teachers that students sue with impunity and believe that they have legal rights to avoid the legitimate decisions of teachers in a classroom.

Go to the professions. The word "profession" comes from the idea of professing values. A profession exists because it's supposed to stand for values of basic honesty and standards of conduct, whether it's in the legal profession, medical profession, accounting profession, or others.

As a practicing lawyer, I don't trust anything another lawyer says or writes. I have seen so many misquotes of cases, so many distortions of facts, that the other lawyer knew were disingenuous, that it has become commonplace to argue whatever you think you can get away with in a crowded courtroom.

A few years ago, I was talking about the state of the profession on a stage in front of 5,000 people in Richmond, Virginia, with several prominent legal scholars. At one point, they started talking about lawyer advertising. They said, "The Supreme Court has held that advertising by lawyers is protected by the First Amendment; therefore, it must be an okay thing; therefore, we should not only accept it but should embrace it. We should have more billboards that say 'WANT TO GET RICH? CALL 1-800-LAWYER'" or whatever we see on the subways and advertised on cable TV shows.

So I said, "Just because it's legal doesn't mean it's ethical. Why don't we treat lawyers who have these disreputable advertisements in a way that shows a lack of respect and not let them in the bar associations and not give them at least some of the courtesies and advantages of being in a profession if they're not professing our values?" At which point, the Harvard law professor on the stage turned to me, dripping with disdain, saying, "What are you going to do, shun them?" I said, "Well, actually, in any profession worthy of the appellation that's exactly that you do. You say that they are disreputable because they don't abide by what you believe are the good values of the legal profession."

Then we go to the public, because it is a big part of the problem here. We've trained everyone to see everything as a matter of individual rights—parents, everyone. They think: "There's a problem; it's a matter of rights." So you have this phenomenon where citizens think that the rights that our Founders gave us to protect freedoms and create a society where we could actually work towards the common good now means grabbing at the common good like it's a dead carcass—"Give me more," pounding on the table.

Ask any principal of a school about this kind of behavior—the threats of lawsuits by parents, to get everything for their child, irrespective of the effects on all the other students in the school.

So what's the solution to this? We have this corrosion that the public generally feels of ethics in our society and civility.

The typical solution is to give a sermon to tell people to be nicer. My father was a preacher. He gave a lot of sermons telling people to be nicer. I never saw that it had much effect, but it was better than not giving a sermon.

President Obama, in his 2011 State of the Union speech, very eloquently called for "a new era of responsibility," where people would wake up in the morning and go forth and not just see things from their selfish point of view but look at everything from the point of view of all of society.

That's incredibly naïve. That isn't how people are. For the reasons stated by Reinhold Niebuhr, among others, people are organs of self-interest. They can justify anything as long as it's in their interest. Many people will do what they can get away with doing.

If we want to restore civility and ethics, we have to have a social structure that allows us to judge people based on civility and ethics.

Talking about responsibility, it is peculiarly a concept that starts at the top, not at the bottom. Only if the teacher has authority to dismiss the disruptive child without paperwork, without proof, without due process hearings, can she maintain control of the classroom. Otherwise the students will learn, as they all have, that they can game the system with impunity because they feel her lack of authority, that she doesn't have the time to actually go through and fill out all those forms and go to the hearings.

Only if the manager actually has the authority to fire someone who's a jerk, who doesn't get along with people or doesn't try hard, will everyone else understand that the culture of this business is that people try hard and they pitch in and they help each other; they don't elbow people out of the way. When's the last time you saw a manager firing somebody for lack of civility or ethical lapses?

In America today, you're not even allowed to give a job reference, speaking of not valuing ethics. That's the rule—my own firm has that rule—because who will protect you if somebody sues and says it was not a good enough reference; or, if you give a good one, that the person wasn't any good. So the rule is everyone just says, "I confirm that So-and-So worked here from this date to this date." That's the rule in America, just like the rule in America is that a teacher can't put an arm around a crying child.

A short while ago, a seven-year-old in Queens was handcuffed because he was disrupting the classroom. The rule is you're not allowed to restrain the student, because they're scared they might get sued or accused of inappropriate touching. So they called the police, and the police led the seven-year-old away in handcuffs. Is that good for the student? That's not uncommon. I could give you 20 stories like that.

If a bar association can't judge lawyers based on the perceptions of their committees on the ethical values of those lawyers, what's the point?

It used to be, when I was a young lawyer, to get into the New York City Bar Association you had to have really legitimate letters of reference; you had to practice for a while. Going to a good school wasn't enough. People had to vouch for your character. Today, all you have to do is prove you have a law degree and you've never been indicted. It's virtually automatic membership.

It's no secret what happened here. We woke up to bad values in the 1960s, and they were bad values—racism, gender discrimination, pollution, ignoring disabled children. One after another, practically every month, there was a new revelation about what we might call abuses of authority in our society.

The solution that we came up with was that we were not going to allow people in responsibility to have authority to assert their values anymore. We were going to lay it out as precisely as possible in law; and, if you couldn't lay it out in law, we would have a legal process where everything would be proved by objective proof. That's where we got due process for ordinary school discipline—you're not sending the kid to jail; you're sending him home. We had this idea that we wanted perfect fairness everywhere.

But it didn't work. It didn't give us good values. It left a vacuum, and the vacuum has been filled by the selfish values of people who figure out how to game the system. Rights, which are our greatest principle for protection against abuses of government authority, have now become a tool of self-interest.

So how do we get this back? We have to restore the authority to act on our values at every level of society. This is going to require a profound legal overhaul in general, replacing bureaucracy with broader principles and individual responsibility.

We need to accept the fact that all choices to do anything in life are human—rules don't make anything happen; only people do. People apply their values either in a good way or in a bad way. There will be people who will assert bad values, and in my system we can hold them accountable for those bad values. But you can't take values away without making everything fail.

Freedom as a formal structure we haven't talked about in a long time, really in our lifetime. But the formal structure is this: law sets boundaries; it tells you what you can't do or you must do—you have to pay your taxes, you can't steal.

But those same boundaries are supposed to affirmatively define and protect an open field of freedom, what the philosopher Isaiah Berlin called "frontiers not artificially drawn within which men shall be enviable." On that open field of freedom people can do whatever they want—they can be jerks, they can have bad values.

Lord Moulton is right, that we can't have law tell people what their values are; that's the antithesis of a free society.

But this open field doesn't work unless law lets us judge other people by their values. They can be jerks, they are free to be jerks, but we are free to judge them. What modern law has done is taken away our freedom to make those value judgments.

It has also taken away the freedom of the people maintaining these boundaries. They can no longer actually assert norms of reasonable behavior, whether it's judges, principals, or anyone else. That has to be restored. Public authority needs to be restored so that people with responsibility have the authority to do their jobs.

Democracy is not supposed to purge our values. Democracy is about asserting values. We want to elect and appoint people who are constantly asserting their values, and if we don't like them, we elect someone else. Instead, we are disempowering everyone, up and down the line.

In the private sector, the same thing. We've got to restore the freedom to judge other people. We do have to protect against discrimination. But discrimination is generally a systemic problem, it's not an individual person problem, so you can safeguard against patterns and practices of discrimination without taking away the ability of employers to write reference letters and to judge people by what they do all day.

And then there's the political system. There is a problem of powerlessness here which I'm doing a lot with. We're just starting a new campaign called

Start Over, which is designed to do a basic overhaul of our regulatory system.

What happens today is Andrew Cuomo goes to Albany to be governor, and he finds that 75 percent of the budget is cast in legal concrete, with deals and statutes made by people who are long dead. He can't change one word of that or shave 5 percent off to balance the budget without getting a majority of the legislature to act.

So there is this extraordinary powerlessness that has come from the accretion of law. It's not that law is doing the wrong goals; it's just you need to do a spring cleaning every once in a while so you're meeting today's goals.

It is not so farfetched to say that democracy today is run by dead people. It's all these laws that have piled up that don't allow anyone—the president can't approve a power line; it would take ten years. You know the smart grid he promised in his campaign? He got to office, he was going to stimulate the economy by spending billions on a new smart grid to create a green infrastructure for America. No way. It will take ten years just to go through the approval process.

The interstate highway system, by contrast, was authorized in an act in 1956 that was 29 pages long, and 14 years later 35,000 miles of road had been built. Today, they would not have been finished with the environmental impact review.

So there is a problem of powerlessness having to do with the accretion of law.

But there is a bigger problem, and it is us. The politicians are appealing to our short-term self-interest.

"I won't touch Medicare." You have to touch it. You don't have to get rid of it. We don't want to get rid of Medicare. I'm close to getting Medicare myself. We don't want to get rid of it. But we have to touch it. We can't afford the health care system so we have to rethink how we organize it.

You can't just keep piling law on top of all these entitlements. We have entitlements from the New Deal, such as cotton subsidies. It's completely absurd.

Our Founders actually made a mistake. They didn't realize that it would be 100 times harder to repeal a law than to pass one. What's happened is the law keeps piling up and no one even talks about repealing the law. But that's because each one of those laws has a special interest and each of us has a special interest.

If we're going to fall for the politics of "let me keep my entitlements/lower my taxes"—which are more or less the two choices we are given—then we are going to get a system that's fundamentally disingenuous and that's never going to solve the problems that we have.

Somehow we have to abandon this politics of self-interest and create an organizational structure where we hold politicians accountable for legitimate proposed solutions to the many challenges of our day, not the pie-in-the-sky rhetoric, hurling accusations back and forth. That's the reason that it's so non-substantive, because they're just appealing to our emotions, not to anything real.

In conclusion, what I wanted and tried to say in this is to get good values in a society, to get civility, we have to have the legal authority to assert them. We also have to have the backbone to assert them, which we don't seem to have in politics.

We don't have the legal authority. It would actually be illegal for the teacher to do things that she needs to do to run a classroom and to imbue her students with good values. We are in a period where we are going to have to fundamentally rethink the legal structure of our society, and that's the only way we're going to get back the America that we all believe in.

★

Henry Kaufman

on

Civility in the Financial Sector

Civility, decency, and high ethical standards are essential not only to social and political life, but for economic and financial progress as well.

Drawing on my rather long experience in the financial markets, and in view of the recent turmoil, I'd like to focus on key aspects of civility and decency; namely, the recurring pattern of irresponsible financial behavior.

Progress in the sciences and technology since the end of World War II has been just astonishing—from moon landings to microcircuits, from modern medicine to the Internet, from bioengineering to nanotechnology.

In contrast, the performance of financial markets has been problematic in many ways. Quantitatively, financial markets have exploded worldwide. The volume and the velocity of securities now traded dwarfs anything that I ever saw in the early career of my life in Wall Street. Yet, we remain subject to regular upheaval, most notably the recent financial crisis, the worst in 80 years.

What is the underlying source of this turmoil? It is not the lack of technological knowledge about how to structure and to trade securities. Rather, it seems to me our financial travail stems mainly from behavioral and ethical shortcomings, from regulatory failures, and from what I would call historical amnesia.

We seem to have learned shockingly little from past financial crises—and there have been many, some dating back many centuries, going back to the 14th century and even earlier.

But that Wall Street has been a problem is, of course, well known. The prevailing culture began to change in the United States.

For a generation or so after World War II, financial behavior was sensible and moderate. The excess of the late 1920s, which many believe led directly to the long collapse that followed, was still fresh in the national consciousness.

More than that, the New Deal regulatory regime had put in place a host of regulatory restraints governing the financial sector and several others. Wall

Street managers and traders generally acted conservatively after World War II in lending and investing practices.

But that prevailing culture began to change as the Depression faded in the memories of many and regulatory restraints were gradually relaxed. From the mid-1960s through the last financial debacle, there have been 15 U.S. financial crises of various sorts and many others around the world.

The 2008 financial crisis is by far the worst in the postwar period. If not for the intervention of the federal government and the Federal Reserve, however belated, many major financial institutions here and abroad would have failed. All were thinly capitalized and interconnected in the markets, and many held huge off-balance-sheet transactions.

How did this irresponsible behavior become so widespread?

One reason was that the financial markets became increasingly depersonalized. One by one, leading investment banks shifted from partnerships to publicly held corporations, while at the same time their relations with clients became more strict and quantitative in nature.

I know from my own experience as a senior partner of Salomon Brothers that the shift from partnership to corporation had profound impacts over time on the level of our risk-taking and in our relationship with clients. I will give you just a couple of examples.

During one of our executive committee meetings back in the 1970s, a young trader interrupted the meeting that was then being held by Bill Salomon, the managing partner, and he gave him a slip informing him of a very large bond trade we had just completed with one of our institutional clients.

Bill asked, "How much did we take out of the trade?"

The young trader replied, "A point," meaning one percentage point.

Bill then called in the partner in charge of transactions, who reaffirmed that the firm had made one point.

Bill Salomon's admonition was brief and to the point. He said, "Salomon Brothers does not take such a profit." The bonds purchased were highly marketable, of high quality, and they were sold by an institution that was a valued client.

He ordered the trading partner to return part of the profit to the institution. In addition, he told the trading partner that the participation in the profits of the firm for him was going to be reduced.

The question then is: What prompted Bill Salomon to take this action in the 1970s? It was, among other things, to protect the relationship with an important institutional client. But it was also to ensure that this wouldn't happen in other transactions of this kind by the firm.

In that era, the strong competitive zeal within Salomon Brothers was tempered by a strong culture of integrity. When the firm became part of a publicly traded corporation named Phibro, the level of risk-taking in trading and positioning securities gradually increased.

This shift from partnership to corporatized Wall Street encouraged the growth of leverage, borrowings. In the earlier period, the owners of the business, the partners, were on-site, and many were actively involved in day-to-day affairs and they had, to use the modern parlance, "considerable skin in the game" which is to say their liability was unlimited.

I will always remember when Sidney Homer, one of my mentors, told me that I would become a partner. He said, "I'm sure that you will rush to tell your wife." Then he added, "But be sure to tell her that once you sign the partnership papers next week you will be personally liable for $2 billion." That was the firm's total liabilities at the time and, therefore, the amount that each partner was personally exposed to.

Many financial institutions—commercial banks, security firms, and insurance companies—took the additional step beyond corporatization to become financial conglomerates.

As they diversified into multiple businesses and grew enormous, their relationship with clients became even more formalized and depersonalized. Highly elaborative quantitative matrices, rather than personal relationships, became much more the norm.

This, in turn, enabled and reinforced the prolif-
eration of new credit instruments and other forms of
securitization, which, in turn, further distanced the
firm from their clients. Securitization, as many of
you have learned by now, the conversion of non-
marketable assets into marketable ones, has been
one of the key factors in excess credit creation and
market behavior. For many of us, the most vivid illustration has been the mortgages that have been
financed in the past ten years or so.

Financial derivatives are another credit instrument
that expanded rapidly in recent decades and contributed massively to excessive credit creation. They too
had a depersonalized influence on markets.

Growing technology interconnected the financial
markets but also fostered an easy credit outlook, as
markets have been linked globally by information
technology and networks, financial information
flows nearly instantaneously, and computerized
trading had spread to more and more exchanges.
Investors can access financial data and participate in
markets around the world and around the clock.

These developments have put many economies
around the world in the cross hairs of financial crisis. In other words, they can be triggered by financial laxities outside the boundaries of any individual
country.

These two developments, securitization and what
is called the seamless interconnectivity of markets,
have brought intricate quantitative risk modeling to

the forefront of financial practices. Securitization, the pricing of securities on a minute-to-minute basis, generates market prices, while information technology offers the power to quantify pricing and risk relationships. The potency of this combination, its effect on risk-taking, cannot be overstated.

Armed with complicated modeling techniques, increasingly powerful computers, and reams of historical market data, a growing number of investors have become entranced with the dream of scientific rectitude. Few recognize, however, that such modeling assumes constancies in market fundamentals. This is because it doesn't take into account structural changes in markets that will affect prices going forward.

For many years I've questioned the wisdom of relying heavily on quantitative risk analysis. The modern quantitative econometric techniques developed since the 1970s have given investors and portfolio managers a new sense of confidence in their ability to forecast future trends and behavior.

The fact is that these relationships don't hold. The vast majority of models rest on assumptions about normal and rational behavior. But during market manias logic doesn't prevail. Such markets are driven more by hubris, elation, fears, pessimism, and the like, which are all emotions that the current models do not, and perhaps cannot, really compute.

So the question is, where does the responsibility lie for the behavior of our financial institutions?

Who is the guardian of credit? The managers of financial institutions, presumably, should be in the front line. But they are as subject to the impact of structural changes in financial markets as any market participant, perhaps even more so.

My first doubt that financial managers would serve as the leading guardian of responsible behavior emerged sometime way back in the 1970s, when securitization, globalization, and new information technology began to filter into the landscape.

I sensed that the conventional wisdom was coming into question when Walter Wriston, the CEO of Citicorp, asked me to come to lunch to discuss a *Financial Times*–sponsored talk I had given about "will the bankers face a harsher climate?" I had concluded that the banks required more equity capital because, among other reasons, the size of their balance sheet was increasing very rapidly.

He disagreed. His conclusion was based on the following premise: first, banks charge floating interest rates on their loans (interest rates go up and down); second, with the gradual deregulation of deposit rates, the cost of bank funds could be managed as a spread below the rate of return on bank assets; and third, because banks could now monitor a constant favorable interest rate spread over the cost of their borrowings, interest rates themselves didn't matter as much as bank managers once feared. For all these reasons, Walter concluded banks did not need to hold as much capital.

Although this argument sounded reasonable, I disagreed and told Walter that for his reasoning to be correct the credit quality of the bank borrower would have to remain constant. Walter was adamant in replying, "Henry, we are bankers and know how to make correct credit judgments." He was of course wrong, which was all the more significant because Walter Wriston was the dominant commercial banker of his era. He was very articulate in writing and in speaking and carried great influence in the financial community

But his comment left an indelible imprint on my thinking, and it helped me to conclude that leaders of financial institutions could not be counted on to be guardians of credit. In fact, the structural changes I've been discussing narrowed the decision-making latitude of senior managers by shifting attention and power to those driven by day-to-day performance pressures—traders, investment bankers, and managers of proprietary trading.

At the same time as financial institutions diversified into new business and new product lines, their senior managers found it increasingly difficult to keep abreast of the vast number of risks in which their firms were investing and trading. It became virtually impossible for them to resist the impulse to grow and compete for profits and market share against rivals who were also taking on a higher risk level. Allow me to give you two examples of how such pressures compromised the judgment of senior financial managers.

The first dates way back into the early 1980s when I was still at Salomon. John Meriwether, who later founded Long-Term Capital Management, came to one of our executive committee meetings and proposed that the firm should become a broker in interest rate swaps. As brokers, we wouldn't be taking any risk because we weren't positioning them.

But several of our competitors soon entered the business. John returned and proposed that we become a dealer. We would take interest swaps into inventory, he explained, but the obligations were of relatively short maturity.

The executive committee again agreed. Within months, we were asked to position much larger and much larger amounts and longer maturities. So the executive committee acquiesced at each step along the way. Trading in interest rate swaps became a very profitable business, and Salomon's risk positioning on these and many other types of derivatives was not very clear. So it wasn't long before the firm's huge level of activity in derivatives began to constrain at times its position in other markets, reflecting a subtle, but quite a significant, shift in Salomon's strategy priorities that grew more and more pronounced over time.

The other illustration is of a more recent vintage. It is a well-known comment in 2007 by Charles Prince, who was the CEO of Citigroup. Referring to his bank's participation in the financial markets, he admitted that "as long as the music is playing, you have to get up on the dance floor and dance."

Now, this insightful comment was quite revealing of how the decision-making process among senior managers of large institutions had become imprisoned. Fear of losing market share, compensation demands by traders and investment bankers, and other short-term competitive pressures made it virtually impossible for top managers to pull their firms off the dance floor. Because their managers' compensation often was linked to their firm's profitability, there was another incentive to stay in the game and lean in favor of greater risk taking.

Damage from financial excesses in recent decades would not have been as severe if not for the aggressive growth in giant financial conglomerates. These institutions played the central role in credit creation through derivatives, mortgage securities, credit default swaps, and other exotic instruments. These firms, which sprawled across commercial banking, investment banking, insurance, credit cards, mutual funds, and many other domains, also embraced quantitative risk analysis, which as I've suggested, tended to increase rather than diminish risk and fostered a debt overload.

Liquidity itself has taken on a new meaning in recent decades. Again, the leading financial conglomerates were at the forefront of the change. Liquidity has shifted from an asset-based concept to one on the liability side of the balance sheet.

Before this shift, corporations measured their liquidity in terms of the inventory turnover, the maturity of accounts receivable, the size of their liquid assets, and of course the relationship of assets to liabilities.

In a couple of decades, a new mindset has emerged in which liquidity is understood to have been access to credit, access to borrowing. Before the recent financial crunch, business began borrowing almost seamlessly and painlessly, and households literally stopped saving when access to credit became super-abundant. The major conglomerates played a heavy and leading role in promoting new mortgage-lending products, flooding the economy with credit cards, and offloading riskier assets into subsidiaries or by securitizing them.

Government officials did not respond promptly to this array of problems created by large financial conglomerates. Even in the wake of the crisis, the reactive Dodd-Frank Act is a rear-guard action designed to build firewalls around large institutions in order to limit the size and scope of their activities.

But these measures, I am convinced, will fail over time. The leading conglomerates already are attempting to chip away at the legislation by lobbying to modify some of the various key elements of the legislation.

In the broadest sense it seems to me that financial consolidation, the concentration of financial assets, affects the foundation of our political economy by pushing us farther away from an ideal economic democracy. As the recent crisis demonstrated vividly, when the financial sector is highly concentrated, the government must continue to play a large role in allocating credit.

Now, just as frailties in economic behavior underlie the drift towards financial concentration, frailties in political behavior help to explain the failure of policymakers to effectively address the "too big to fail" conundrum.

Neither major party was eager to support measures that would genuinely support financial competition and ensure the dominance of market mechanisms in credit allocation.

Of course, identifying which firms are "too big to fail" is a tricky business. Still, if the largest diversified financial institutions were required to divest assets, competition, by definition, would increase in the universe of our credit markets. But lack of political will on both sides of the aisle ensured that the Dodd-Frank Act did not address the "too big to fail" issue decisively. It effectively kicked the can down the road, leaving it to others to deal with it and the ultimate negative consequences of heavy concentration.

Foundationally, the responsibility of guarding our financial system resides for the most part with the Federal Reserve System. Charged with encouraging economic growth and price stability, the Fed has the power to raise and to lower interest rates.

Its performance record has been checkered. In responding to the 2008 crisis, the Fed response was late, but nevertheless massive, dramatic, and I thought, innovative. That intervention stopped the economy and the financial markets from falling into an abyss. Even the much-debated quantitative easing you've been reading about was from my perspective correct, because it reversed the decline in the value of financial assets, an important prerequisite for reversing the weakness in the economy.

Although the central bank response to the crisis was generally admirable, its role leading up to the crisis was much more problematic. Up until the crisis was in full bloom, the Federal Reserve took a hands-off approach in managing the credit structure of the United States. It followed a kind of a clinical and antiseptic tactic of focusing on the growth of the monetary variables and, thus, failed to adequately restrain the growth of credit, the growth of debt. It allowed credit and debt to grow much faster than the growth of the economy's nominal GDP.

As I have suggested, the rapid growth of credit in recent decades was propelled, of course, by several structural changes in the financial markets and a lot of innovation. Officials at the Federal Reserve failed to appreciate the impact of these changes—securitization, derivative growth, and so on—and to understand what the impact would be on the economy and the system.

The Fed failed also to recognize that abandoning the Glass-Steagall Act would accelerate financial concentration and thereby create even more of a "too big to fail" problem. It took the near-collapse of our financial system for the Fed to officially admit in public that some giant institutions were too big to fail.

The Fed's role as a guardian of our financial system is analogous to the relationship between the parent and a child. As a guardian, the parent's role is to set out standards of behavior and hold the child to those standards. A parent should not play the role of a friend in his or her relationship with the child. Similarly, the central bank should define and enforce standards of behavior. It should never become a folk hero of the marketplace.

I would take it even a step further. No senior government official dealing with supervision of financial markets should be permitted to be employed by financial institutions within several years after leaving the government of the United States.

I'd be a little bit remiss in my comments on the current irresponsible financial behavior if I failed to comment on the role of the economics profession.

On the whole, this role has been less than distinguished.

As noted academic economists became entranced with trying to mathematically move ahead by modeling economic behavior, the theory of rational expectations became extremely popular in the halls of academia.

Two recent critics of this describe it as follows: "An economic theory of the world that starts from the premise that nothing genuinely new ever happens has a particularly simple—and thus attractive—mathematical structure: Its models are made up of fully specified mechanical rules that are supposed to capture individual decision-making and market outcomes at all times: past, present, and future." [Roman Frydman and Michael D. Goldberg, *Beyond Mechanical Markets: Asset Price Swings, Risk, and the Role of the State* (Princeton University Press, 2011)].

The popularity of the theory of rational expectation and the concomitant quantification of economic and financial behavior encouraged the academic community to downplay the importance of structural changes and the impact on the economy and financial markets. There were precious few academic economists who called attention to the instability of our financial system.

Academicians and private-sector economists alike are heavily influenced by behavioral biases that are very difficult to escape. On the whole, these biases discourage analysts and market participants from accepting the likelihood of panics, crises, and other financial mishaps.

Consider for example the all-too-human propensity to minimize risk and to avoid isolation. It is comforting to run in the crowd, and doing so minimizes the likelihood of being singled out or being wrong.

When it comes to looking ahead, we inescapably look to the past for guidance. But it is important to keep in mind that history never repeats itself, but rather, as Mark Twain said, it rhymes. This makes the real challenge to identify what differs from the past in the current situation, quite a difficult challenge. Mathematical equations that are based on historical data are unable to make such judgments.

Another important cognitive bias is that most of us find it very difficult to actually change our minds. Consider the economist who gained prominence through years of writing and developing an economic and financial theory. This economist is unlikely to change his conclusions promptly in light of contrary evidence. And this is probably true for anyone working beyond the confines of a test-tube.

There is also a clear bias against negative predictions. As far as I know, no American president, no chairman of the Council of Economic Advisers, no secretary of the U.S. Treasury or chairman or the Federal Reserve has ever forecast a business recession.

For that matter, large business and financial institutions avoid talk of near-term difficulties. The latest financial turmoil was, of course, no exception to this bias. Just months before the crisis reached its depth in 2008, officials noted publicly that the problem in the housing market was "well contained."

There are many reasons for this bias, not least the fact that negative economic and financial projections make for bad politics. They can cut short the career of political leaders, interfere with the aspirations of leaders in business and in finance, and imperil the performance record of financial managers, even when they are on the mark.

How many times have we heard prominent individuals say in response to some negative development: "Of course I am a long-term optimist. This too will pass."

Of course most of us here and everywhere are optimists. How else would we cope with the many harsh realities of life?

I have personally encountered the fallout that comes to those who make negative predictions. Decades ago, I was labeled "Doctor Doom." Indeed, the economist Albert Wojnilower, a friend of mine of many years, was called "Doctor Death."

What did I warn about that earned me this title of Doctor Doom? My major concern included the dangerous rise in the rate of inflation in the 1970s, the excessive speculation and speculative zeal of markets and market financial participants, the over-leveraging by financial institutions and business corporations, and the periodic ineptness of official policymakers.

Economists and business analysts, especially those employed by "sell-side institutions"—that is, organizations involved in such activities as trading and investment banking—are confronted with the difficult task of maintaining objectivity. Just the designation of "sell-side" suggests that their analysis should help further a trade or the distribution of new securities. Wall Street has been riddled with this conflict, which has become more and more exposed in recent decades.

To minimize this conflict, I feel strongly that the head of research should be a member of the senior management and not report to the head of an operating function, such as trading, sales, or investment banking. That is still not the process.

At Salomon Brothers, the role I eventually attained on the executive committee afforded me independence from sell-side and other pressures and did give me the opportunity to shelter the research effort of the firm. When in the 1980s I came to disagree with Salomon's new strategy decisions that I feared would get it into trouble, I didn't take any pleasure in severing the longtime relationship or in the fact that the firm got into difficulties later on.

My point is that very few members of the investment community enjoy the kind of independence from conflict of interest that I enjoyed, and we should do all that we can to minimize such pressure and biases.

For all the advanced econometric modeling and other new techniques at the disposal of today's economists, they are not observing a world as reliably predictable as experts in the physical sciences and cannot run the same kind of controlled experiments. Theirs is a human science.

I wish I could assure you that irresponsible behavior in financial markets will abate in the future. But I can't.

As we struggle to emerge in the aftermath of the recent upheavals, we continue to face some headwinds. Far too many financial assets are still not shown on the books at realistic prices. Oversight in both the United States and in Europe remains under par and still has to be agreed upon. Occasionally, near-term speculative impulses in financial markets continue to flare, but they will be constrained for a while by the massive debt overhang in the credit structure.

We need fundamentally new ways of thinking about market behavior from our economic thinkers and political leaders. It is so difficult for those who have dominated economic thought and dominated political life in recent decades—and still do—to think in fundamentally new ways.

The new paradigms almost certainly will emerge not from the minds of the incumbents, but rather from the ranks of tomorrow's leaders.

★

Steve Forbes

on

Civility in Corporate America

It's a great pleasure talking about civility. Let me first hit the political side of things, and then I'll talk about what's happening regarding people's feelings on ethics and fair rules in the economy and corporate America.

On the political side, there is obviously a feeling that civility has declined, especially with the fighting in Washington, D.C., which, since Watergate, has been more *ad hominem*.

You saw it in the attacks on Bill and Hillary Clinton and those attacks on Sarah Palin. Putting aside your political views of these people, the personal attacks certainly overstepped a lot of bounds.

You can see it in the fights over Supreme Court appointees, starting with Robert Bork in the late 1980s. Pure trash and misrepresentation.

You saw a graphic example of this recently, when Congressman Paul Ryan of Wisconsin came up with a proposal to reform Medicare. Whether you agree or disagree with his approach, it was a very thoughtful proposal. He knows a lot about entitlements. Sitting in the audience, the President of the United States got up and trashed Ryan. And the Democrats ran ads of a grandmother being thrown over a cliff. Ryan's proposal makes no changes to Medicare in the next ten years, and those already on or going on Medicare during the next ten years are not affected by his reforms at all.

People feel things are unraveling, and there are several factors at work on the political side.

I mentioned Watergate, where the fighting went way beyond the specific facts at hand and got personal. For some reason Richard Nixon was a catalyst for very intense personal animosities. So the positions on both sides became personal and were very sharp edged.

We also live in a world in which, thanks to changes in technology and media, the tools for discourse encourage loudness. You see this with talk radio, where there are call-ins—that's great for dialogue, but people can mouth off in a way that normally you'd save for the corner bar yet somehow feel free to express over the airwaves.

The Web makes everything instant and makes everyone able to communicate with one another. So now we have verbal inquisitions of candidates and office-holders. Party purists can go after you in ways that were never possible before.

Another factor is that there are many new voices. More new groups and people are participating in the public square, and one way you get heard is by raising your voice. So it's a reflection of the raucousness of our democracy. It's a high-tech version of what we saw during Andrew Jackson's presidency and the changes in politics during the 1820s, when a whole new slate of people got actively involved in the public square.

In terms of today's new groups, they all want to do fund-raising. And when you fund-raise you have to write your fund-raising appeals in an apocalyptic voice: "Coat hangers are coming back"; "Washington is going to knock on your door at midnight"; "You're going to be destroyed financially." So this apocalyptic vision also ups the ante, intensifies things. And, because there's so much more of it than before, we notice the volume of it in a way that we hadn't previously.

Another factor is the size of government. When you have big government, one of the things that comes in its wake—certainly in this country—is that congressional staffs and offices get bigger. So even if you're a mere congressperson, you now have your own little fiefdom, your own little bubble. So even in the evenings, when you might have had a drink with your colleagues—now you're off to fundraisers instead.

The work week in Washington is very strange. If you're in the national legislature, it's Tuesday through Thursday. You return to Washington Monday night and leave Thursday night to go back and do constituent work. So the normal ways of reducing the edges, of interacting with your colleagues, have been reduced. At committee hearings you're in and out. If you've ever been to a committee hearing, unless someone's done something egregiously wrong and *The Washington Post* and others are interested in it, you'll notice that there are one or two people there and everyone else comes in and out, asks a question and then goes off to their next thing.

Just about the only time people interact is at the gyms. We saw that—and this is the exception that proves the rule—when Senator Coburn of Oklahoma got to know then Senator Barack Obama, and they established a relationship. It hasn't led to much in terms of a compromise or grand agreement, but at least the President feels very free to call Coburn and lecture him on what he sees as the evils and ills of some GOP position. He doesn't do that with many other Republicans. He doesn't feel comfortable picking up the phone and letting loose with: "Your party, blah, blah, blah."

Just one little side comment: Most of the time in the House and Senate things are boringly civil. You don't say much there; that's not where the action is.

In contrast, the rudeness in the U.K. on the floor of Parliament is legendary. And thanks to C-SPAN, you can see it. Somebody gets up to speak and everyone says, "You're a fool, sit down." They don't hesitate to interrupt. But once off the floor, there are civil rules that are observed.

As for other countries, you often see fistfights in South Korea and Japan. You don't have to watch HBO to see extreme fighting. In Taiwan the legislature is notorious; they throw chairs at each other. Talk about ultimate wrestling.

But the real reason for all the raucousness on the political side—which spills over to the economic side—is that while there are new tools and new voices, there also are very fundamental differences over many issues. And when there are fundamental differences, with no real consensus, passions rise. And with human nature being what it is, when passions rise, normal civil debate is forgotten. When people feel that the stakes are high, passions are inflamed.

Take the social issue of abortion. Wherever you stand on this, your position is passionately held. I've got scar tissue from that from my own presidential runs. People have passionate feelings about abortion, and hearing certain words will make them go off. We see the same thing playing out now over gay marriage. So on issues that people feel passionately about, don't be surprised when the discourse isn't carried out in terms of Socratic debates with questions and answers.

The economy: What should be the size and role of government? For most of our history the only interaction people had with the federal government was through the post office.

When you look at the history of Europe—except for Britain, which was an exception—the rise of warfare meant that you had to have a stronger and stronger central government, hence the absolute monarchs in Spain and in France. When there was an uprising in France, such as the Fronde in the 1600s, the center won. Louis XIV never forgot it. He eviscerated the aristocracy and sent it out to do nothing in Versailles.

England did not have a strong center. So when it had a civil war, the other side won. When the monarchy was restored, it was a neutered monarchy, with Parliament holding the power.

During the American Civil War, there was a massive increase in government powers. But after the war, such things as income tax were repealed, and things went back to the way they had been before. The same with the First World War. There was a massive increase in government powers, including nationalizing the Post Office and the telephone industry. After the war, things were denationalized. During the 1920s the size of government was sharply reduced, the national debt was reduced and the income tax rate was cut from 77% to 25%.

There have been periods before in our history when people have felt passionately about issues. I mentioned the Civil War. You all know the story of Senator Charles Sumner, from Massachusetts, a fierce abolitionist, who was nearly killed on the floor of the Senate by an angry congressman who beat Sumner almost to death with a cane.

When people feel strongly about moral issues, they don't compromise. At the time leading up to the war, more and more people felt you couldn't compromise on slavery; Southerners felt they couldn't compromise on what they saw as their way of life. And so, as Abraham Lincoln said, the war came.

The 1790s, at the beginning of our republic, was probably one of the most vicious periods, in terms of a lack of civility. We think of our Founders as wise people—and they were. They were brilliant, but they were also very human. After the Constitution was passed and we started our new government, everyone knew that precedents were going to be set on policies made. Therefore the stakes were very high, and issues were viciously, passionately fought over.

Once upon a time—when we were taught history in this country—we all learned about the fight between Thomas Jefferson and Alexander Hamilton.

Jefferson, for all of his virtues, had a very static, agrarian view of society. Adams said that Hamilton was the "bastard brat of a whore"—which tells you how Adams felt about Hamilton. But Hamilton, precisely because he was born out of wedlock and because he had come to this country at a fairly young age, was not attached to a colony, not attached to family. To him mobility was absolutely key, as was manufacturing, and he loved the idea of money. To Hamilton money was the way to mobility. It didn't matter if the patriarch of the town liked you or not—if you had money, it was the great equalizer. His beliefs were the antithesis of Jefferson's.

The Jeffersonians thought that everything about the new financial system Hamilton put in, such as the national bank, undermined the agrarian ideal and brought in the evils of the cities and commerce. This was passionately fought over. Thomas Jefferson was very adept with his poison pen and knew how to hire poison penners, including a fellow named James Callender, to trash the opposition. But when Jefferson had a falling-out with him, Callender got the ultimate revenge against Jefferson: He let out the story of Jefferson's relations with Sally Hemings, a slave. And that's what most people remember about Jefferson today.

So infighting in the government is not new.

The 1930s saw a huge break in American tradition in terms of the role of government. I'm getting at this in a long-winded way, but this is very important, as it's still being played out today.

The lesson people took away from the Depression? If you leave free markets alone, bad things will happen.

In 1929, the United States had the largest, most sophisticated economy in the world. In contrast with other developed countries in the world, however, the size of the U.S. government was only 3% of GDP, state and local government maybe 6 or 7%. This was very small by European or even British standards.

Small government was very much part of the American, the Hamiltonian tradition. Government did certain things and then got out of the way.

But in 1929 the Great Depression hit. Herbert Hoover is often portrayed as a do-nothing President. In actuality he was a very activist President. He didn't have good spin, and he was awkward and stiff in the public square. But in terms of doing things, no President before him had done more than he did. And Franklin Roosevelt put those doings on steroids.

But what animated the response to the Depression was the experience people had had during World War I. There was a progressive tradition in this country, and there was the feeling that science should be brought into politics, that experts could run things better than the masses of ignorant people who voted.

For an intense period of time during World War I, the government took on massive amounts of power to wage the war. Even Franklin Roosevelt, who was, in effect, as assistant secretary of the Navy, running the Navy, found this a heady experience. The feeling was: "If we could use the powers of government to win a war, and we have science at our fingertips, by golly we can lick this Depression and not by going back to the old way where you step back and let the thing heal by itself. We're going to take an activist approach."

So we had an enormous peacetime increase in government powers. Take the National Recovery Administration for instance, which was almost statist, fascistic, in its sweep. Businesspeople got together from each industry and wrote codes determining what prices could be charged and what working conditions had to exist. If you violated those codes, you could be imprisoned. And people were. A tailor went to jail because he charged only 30 cents to press a suit, instead of 40 cents, per the code. There was the notorious case of the chicken plucker who sold chickens. However, customers were not supposed to be able to pick out a live chicken; they had to do it blind. This guy let customers pick out their own chickens. He was arrested and put in jail.

In 1935 the Supreme Court threw all these regulations out. But the idea of the government taking an activist approach in keeping the economy on an even keel had already taken root.

In the late 1930s the government started to decline a little bit. But then came the Second World War. And when a country is engaged in total war the government must take on massive amounts of powers.

After World War II—we often forget—government sharply declined in this country. But then came the Cold War—and again, everything revolved around warfare. Even building the National Highway System, which President Eisenhower started in the 1950s, was seen as a national defense measure. The government followed this with getting involved in education—not because education is good, but because we had to have an educated workforce to compete against the Soviet Union. Thus government grew and grew.

Conservatives were faced with a paradox: They don't like big government, but if they wanted to wage a war—cold or hot—they had to accept a big government. Something we should have learned from studying the absolute monarchies in Western Europe.

By the end of the Cold War government had achieved size and scope. The debate then became very passionate: How big should government be?

Ideology takes on religious fervor. We always wonder how the Spanish could have the Inquisition, how they could burn people at the stake. We don't physically burn people today, but we do it verbally if someone strays from a certain viewpoint. And no quarter is given.

Take the health care debate. Again this goes back to the response to the Depression: What should the role of government be? Some people have the vision of the government as being the answer to everything. In this case it would provide, in effect, a one-payer system for everybody—"It works in Europe, why can't it work here?" Others feel that this is postalizing health care, which will lead to horrors and a decline in health care research.

You see this in education. Those who believe in government education see it as egalitarian, making sure we have a properly educated workforce. Philip Howard, whom you've heard from as part of this series, talks about how public education today is almost as bad as the IRS Income Tax Code, with all the rules and regulations teachers and administrators must follow. So you have those who say "don't touch the education system; leave it alone; or just give it more money." Others feel there should be more charter schools, more choice, that we should open the system up, and try to create more accountability. By the way, regarding that debate, Joel Klein, the former chancellor for the New York City Department of Education, wrote a very interesting article in the June 2011 issue of *The Atlantic*, in which he said the education system—certainly that in New

York and in some other areas he's familiar with—is about the adults, not the children. That's a very telling statement.

All these issues ignite fierce debate. Anytime you try to tamper with education budgets, passions rise enormously.

But this also occurs regarding the economy itself.

Take energy. Should the government, in effect, force us to use what it thinks is a good source of energy? It is now mandating what kind of light bulbs we can use. But the light bulb is only a symbol of the fierce debate about where we should go regarding energy.

You see it in the management of the economy. John Maynard Keynes truly believed that wise people could manage an economy. Whatever brilliance Keynes had, he was oblivious to the fact that in government there is politics, and how people weigh in, in terms of what they think should or should not be done, is influenced by who is helped and who is not.

The Federal Reserve believes that it can guide the economy. Others passionately believe that the Federal Reserve just gums things up. Liberals see free markets as inherently unstable; conservatives believe that, with sensible rules of the road and if the government gets out of the way, free markets work.

There is no consensus on energy or on social issues, not to mention on entitlements—and a huge debate is coming there. And it should be no surprise when passions become inflamed.

This is happening in Greece. I was there recently, and there was tear gas filling my hotel's lobby. We haven't yet experienced that in this country. But when the debates are fierce ones, you get fierce passions.

Which brings me to a quick point I want to make. When the value of money becomes unhinged, it undermines social rules, people's sense of there being guardrails and fairness in the marketplace. John Maynard Keynes got one thing profoundly right. He said that the most destructive social force is debasing the value of money, because it brings about all the forces of social destruction. But he said that not one in a million people understand the process. He said Lenin understood it, which is why Lenin trashed the ruble; he was out to destroy the old order.

In the 1970s Americans became a nation of consumers. Why? Because saving was for suckers. You put aside money for an annuity, but the real value of your annuity was destroyed. And even though inflation was conquered in the early 1980s, the aftermath is still being felt.

Eight years ago our Federal Reserve, for its own reasons, started the money printing presses again. Other central banks around the world had to follow suit, as did the euro and the pound. When there's a creation of excess money, it eventually leads to a profound belief that the rules of the game have gone by the boards. And when you have that kind of inflation, the money goes into commodities. Why? To preserve the value of what you have. It goes to physical things. This is why we have seemingly unfair profits in the oil industry—the windfall profits of the 1970s, "evil oil." Today there's again the feeling that these people are not playing by the rules, that they're shafting us.

The same holds true for Wall Street. Wall Street could not have had its recent outsize profits had the government not created too much money. There would never have been a housing bubble without that excess money.

So traditional flows of capital become unhinged. People feel that the rules of the game are stacked, that they're getting too much for too little effort, that there's no real link between reward and effort. Keynes was right: When this happens people feel unmoored, and that raises fears, which raises passions.

There's a populist tinge to this, whether you're going after bankers, Wall Streeters, evil oil company executives or businesspeople in general. This atmosphere reinforces the old caricature of businesspeople. As you know, in Hollywood movies business executives have killed more people than serial killers have. They are either portrayed as heavily jowled and pleased by the misery they're causing or they're Scrooge-like—scrawny and skinny, with long fingers. And they're all plotting to poison the water and kill people's pets. That sort of thing.

Both government and the private sector have got to get this currency thing right. When the value of money fluctuates, it plays to people's worst instincts, but when free markets are allowed to work with sensible rules of the road…. James Madison, the father of our Constitution, was absolutely right when he said that if we were angels we would not need government, and if angels were ruling us we would not need checks and balances. But, manifestly, we're not angels. So we do need rules, we do need laws, we do need government. But the question is: What kind of rules? That's the fierce debate we're experiencing today.

When there is inflation, activities occur in which there seems to be no connection between effort and reward, innovation and reward. Here are a couple of quick things to keep in mind regarding free markets.

To succeed in a free market you must provide a product or service that somebody else wants or needs. It's all about meeting the needs and wants of other people. For example, if 12 years ago you had said the word "iPod," people would be wondering if you were talking about a remake of a movie about alien pod people. Steve Jobs expanded on the concept of the old Sony Walkman—which should have evolved into the iPod had Sony taken it to the next step. Suddenly, we decided we couldn't live without these things. Same with iPhones, iPads and everything else.

I'm old enough to remember when Xerox copiers came along and suddenly we couldn't live without those. And if you go to a dinner party today, half the people will have their heads down, getting their instant fix and needing to keep in touch (literally and figuratively) on their iPhones.

In a free market, if you don't meet the needs and wants of other people, you'll fail, you won't succeed. This breeds its own kind of civility. We think of markets as greedy, as impersonal, as trying to euchre you out of your hard-earned money. But keep in mind what free markets do without your realizing it; they force you to pay attention to other people, to know your customer. If you don't know your customer, you might get in trouble. Without our realizing it, ever-wider webs of chains of cooperation are bred because nobody's in charge.

Here's one example of just how complex supply chains have become. I mentioned the iPhone. The iPhone comes from China. It costs $178, with the parts in it, when it comes into this country. Obviously, you're charged more than that. Out of that $178, only $6.50 of those parts are actually manufactured in China. The rest are assembled from numerous areas around the world, including Germany, Japan (one reason that Apple's stock took a hit after the natural disasters in Japan earlier this year where a lot of Apple's parts come from), South Korea, and, amazingly, the United States. So if you look at the $178, you say, "Oh my God, the U.S. has a $178 trade deficit with China." If you look at the actual manufactured parts, $6.50's worth is from China, but 10 dollars' worth of that $178 phone is actually parts made in the U.S., shipped to China, put in the iPhone and shipped back to the U.S.

Ever more sophisticated supply chains breed ever more sophisticated financial services. Banks have gained their current scope not just because they're greedy and trying to control the world but also because they're meeting the needs of the marketplace and the absolute chains of specialization.

Adam Smith said that markets are all about transactions. You go to a restaurant because you want food; the restaurant wants your money. It gives you food; you give them money. It's an exchange.

There are a lot of exchanges we don't like. Nobody likes paying rent; nobody likes paying the electricity bill. But you do get something in return. Human nature being what it is, those who complain the loudest about paying the electricity bill don't hesitate to go out and spend $200 on a pair of blue jeans that look as if they came out of a Dumpster. Go figure.

Free markets are imperfect because people are imperfect. But, as with free elections, you don't throw them out because there is also fraud. You deal with the specific problems. The overall system is about as good as you're going to get in this world.

The same is true of free markets: You deal with the specific problems; you don't chuck the whole thing out because there are flaws.

Unfortunately, in the current debate the choice seems to be either suffocating government regulation or anarchy. Again, sensible rules of the road should prevail.

Even though for the next couple of years things will be even more raucous than they are today, there are a couple of things that are going to get worked out.

One is that we will eventually get the money situation right. Here's a prediction: Five years from now the dollar—for the first time since the 1970s—is going to be relinked to gold.

Once we again have a global system of stable money, you'll start to see commerce thrive. There'll be more prosperity, and that will lower the temperature enormously, once people feel that there's a link again between effort and reward. A properly run system provides both stability and—history clichés to the contrary—flexibility. So this will help.

Another thing that will help—which may sound strange—is our political system. Even the much-maligned Electoral College actually helps keep this country together. To win national office in this country you have to put together coalitions of people who may not like each other much or even share a lot of common ground. To give you an example: In Iowa, the Republican Party is very concerned with social issues. If you're not to the right on social issues, you don't fare well in Iowa. But in New Hampshire—same country, same language, same party—for the most part people don't give a hoot about social issues. You'll find more pro-life Republicans in New Hampshire than you will pro-life Democrats in New York. As long as you don't tax people and take their guns away, New Hampshirites don't get too concerned over social issues—economic issues, yes, but social issues, no.

So, same country, same language and same party, but two very different focuses. Yet they are part of the whole. As I said, you cannot win high national office here without putting together seemingly disparate groups of people.

This can lead, paradoxically, to things being watered down to mush. Only once has the system failed, but that was because of the profound moral issue of slavery during the Civil War. Most of the time the system keeps this heterogeneous country functioning. We have two major political parties that share some broad generalities, but their focus is very different in areas around the country. Yet having to build a consensus brings them together. The only way a President is going to get elected is by putting all these disparate groups together, otherwise, with the way the Electoral College works, you won't succeed.

In the next five years we'll see the emergence of a new consensus. We can debate what that consensus will be. But this country always has had a knack for rising above periods when there's been profound disruption from economic change or how people view the world. Somehow things come together and life goes on, and the country holds together.

We will rise again from this period of incivility and seeming instability. On the economic side—at least in a broad sense—we'll get things right so people won't feel that the link between effort and reward has been disrupted, that the markets are unfair. As for the political side, we'll hash things out. Bismarck was right. He said there are two things people shouldn't see being made: sausages and laws. Now, because of transparency, everyone is involved in making laws, so it's a very messy process. But it will sort itself out.

★

John Brademas

on

Civility in Public Life

I would like to offer some observations from my own service in Congress, as well as the current state of politics, and offer a few modest recommendations for improving civility in the public sphere.

I was for 22 years, from 1959 to 1981, a member of the United States House of Representatives. I served with six presidents, three Republicans, Eisenhower, Nixon, Ford, and three Democrats, Kennedy, Johnson, Carter. In Congress I served on three committees: Education and Labor, House Administration, and the Joint—that is to say, House-Senate—Committee on the Library of Congress. I took an active part in writing the Elementary and Secondary Education Act, the Education for All Handicapped Children Act, Head Start, college student aid, and the legislation creating the National Endowment for the Arts and the Humanities, the Arts and Artifacts Indemnity Act, and measures to support libraries and museums. In my last four years in Congress, I was, by appointment of the speaker, Tip O'Neill, the majority whip of the House, No. 3 in the Democratic Party leadership.

After 22 years of service in the United States House of Representatives, I was, in my campaign for a 12th term, defeated in Ronald Reagan's landslide victory over President Carter. Shortly thereafter, I was invited to become president of New York University, a position in which I served until 1992, when I became president emeritus, my present position. My principal project now is the John Brademas Center for the Study of Congress, which examines the roles of Congress as a policymaking institution. I remind you that in our separation-of-powers constitutional system, when it comes to making national policy, Congress—unlike the House of Commons, for example, in the British parliamentary system—counts. If a senator or representative knows what he or she is doing and if the configuration of political forces makes action possible, that senator or representative can, without picking up the telephone to call the White House, write the laws of the land.

With 100 senators and 435 representatives, and normally no strict party discipline, Congress is not an easy institution to understand, even for informed persons. Located in NYU's Robert F. Wagner Graduate School of Public Service, our center engages senators and representatives, current and former, Democrats and Republicans—this is not a partisan issue—congressional staffers, journalists, students and scholars to discuss the processes, the ways by which our national legislature influences and shapes policy, as well as significant issues of public policy. By encouraging the exchange of ideas among scholars and policymakers, the center promotes the creation and dissemination of knowledge and public understanding of what is, after all, the first branch of government.

Let me say that it would be a mistake simply to dismiss our current state of affairs and look longingly back to a time when politics was marked by its civility, because we risk becoming nostalgic for a more civil time that may never have really existed. I myself served in Congress in the era of the fight for civil rights legislation and the terrible divisions over the Vietnam War. I was there on the floor of the 1968 Democratic Convention in Chicago, where members of my own delegation, the Indiana delegation, were shouting one another down and refusing to recognize speakers, not to mention the riots going on outside.

I was the principal author of a bill, the Comprehensive Child Development bill, which passed with strong bipartisan support in the House of Representative—the bill then was vetoed by President Nixon. In a demagogic veto message, Nixon accused Walter Mondale, my coauthor in the Senate, and me of trying to collectivize the American family, impugning communist motivation to our attempt to provide federal support on a voluntary basis for child care.

Needless to say, when Nixon's enemies list was reported by the press, I was congratulated by my colleagues on the House floor for the honor of having achieved a spot on it.

Yet during this era of civil rights, Vietnam, and Watergate, I was privileged to serve with some of the finest public servants—Birch Bayh, William Fulbright, Jacob Javits, Ted Kennedy, Tip O'Neill. In times of terrible divisiveness in the country and in Congress, we worked together, Republicans and Democrats, to create enduring programs and institutions, from Medicare to the National Endowment for the Arts, from the Peace Corps to the Apollo space program. The pieces of legislation I'm most proud of having worked on—the Education for All Handicapped Children Act and the Arts and Artifacts Indemnity Act—were passed by Democratic congresses and signed into law by a Republican president, Gerald Ford.

My point here is that while there may be no golden age of civility in politics, perhaps we can still learn some lessons from how, even during periods of tragedy, division, and conflict in American society and politics, leaders could still find common ground and identity and work together on important issues.

One of the biggest changes since the time I was in the House is the weakening of the congressional committee system. I arrived on Capitol Hill when committees and their chairmen were nearly all-powerful, and the old Southern Democrats who chaired many committees used their positions to kill any civil rights legislation, even when it would have had the support of a majority of the House. It took President Johnson, using up the political capital he gained from his landslide victory in 1964, finally to bypass these old bulls and push the Civil Rights Act through Congress.

So I am not calling for a return to an era when committee chairs exercised absolute control over legislation, but I did serve at a time when commit-tees played a greater and more positive role. Com-mittees had adequate staff resources. We held hear-ings, not just for show on C-SPAN and cable news, but seriously to get input from witnesses as we crafted legislation and to build support among con-stituents for a bill. By working out legislation in committee and by having Republican and Democ-ratic staffers working together, it often—I won't say always—helped produce legislation that was built on consensus, with input from more junior members and from both sides of the aisle.

When I was chairman of the Subcommittee on Education and working on a bill, I would ask the ranking Republican member, Al Quie of Minnesota, whom he would like invited to testify before the subcommittee. I didn't have to do this, but it was an effective way to build trust and cooperation between the Democrats and the Republicans on the committee. Then, when it came time to marking up a bill, I would turn to Quie and say, "Al, what do you need on this bill to vote for it?"

So while a bill we reported may not have been one my Republican colleagues would ever have written themselves, it contained ideas they offered and was a measure they could support.

But beginning with the Republican takeover of Congress in 1994, the trend has been to consolidate power in the leadership at the expense of committees. Unfortunately, this trend was not reversed when the Democrats again took control of Congress in 2006, and it continues today. The cutting of resources, such as reductions in committee staff and elimination of the research offices, has meant more and more reliance on lobbyists, who provide research and even the language of a bill. The most important legislation is now written in the leadership office. The speaker and majority and minority leaders from each chamber then appoint the conferees who hash out the final bill between the House and Senate. Then the leadership moves the final bill through the floors for passage.

Committees are often relegated to the role of by-standers in this process.

The result has been more and more omnibus bills and attaching non-germane items to so-called "must-pass" bills, such as Defense Department appropriations, in order to get them through the Senate. I am the child of the House, so I'm afraid I have few specific recommendations for improving that more peculiar chamber, the Senate.

Although our topic is now civility, I'm reminded of an old story of when I was on Capitol Hill during a bitter floor fight on a piece of legislation. A freshman Democratic member of the House was talking with a more senior member when the freshman referred to the Republicans as "the enemy."

"Never call Republicans the enemy," he admonished his junior colleagues. "They are the opposition. It's the Senate that is the enemy."

We are, in fact, looking at a Senate which, if the current trend of votes this year continues, is on track to being one of the least productive when measured in numbers of votes taken, bills passed, and appointments confirmed.

One recommendation I do have is for the Senate to pass the Presidential Appointment Efficiency and Streamlining Act, which has been reported by the Government Affairs Committee and is awaiting action by the full Senate. The act would remove from Senate confirmation around 200 positions from executive branch departments and agencies that are not involved in policymaking or budget decisions. Hundreds of presidential appointments currently require Senate confirmation, and nominees languish for months waiting for votes, leaving offices in departments and agencies without leadership and discouraging qualified persons from serving.

Individual senators have been loath to give up their leverage afforded by the ability to hold up a confirmation, holding a nominee hostage to extract concessions from the White House on unrelated matters. Passing this act would be a good first step at reform and improving civility in the appointments and confirmation process.

I served at a time before BlackBerries and cell phones and when air travel was such that members were not able to get back regularly to their home districts. Now, for good or bad, electronic devices keep senators and representatives in constant contact, not just with family at home, but with staff and media, and the congressional calendar is designed so that members can work midweek on the Hill and then fly home for three or four days over the weekend. Senators and representatives are constantly working, whether in Washington or their districts, but they are spending far less time, professionally and socially, with each other.

The Brademas Center recently brought to NYU former senators Trent Lott and Tom Daschle. Lott and Daschle served as the Democratic and Republican leaders in the Senate during the late 1990s and early 2000s, and then went back and forth between the majority and minority during that time, neither ever approaching a filibuster-proof majority.

Yet during these years, despite their significant differences in policy, they both worked together to get the business of the Senate done. Neither punitively gummed up the works of the Senate when they were in the minority. What they both gave the most credit to in how they worked to get legislation moved through the chamber and appointments confirmed—and I assure you that the record of the Senate since their departure as leaders has gone downhill in these areas—was their personal friendship. Senators Lott and Daschle would speak every day, either in person or by phone. They and their wives would go to dinner together. They stressed how this friendship prevented them from impugning the motives of the other and created an atmosphere of cooperation even in the face of such difficult circumstances as the impeachment trial of President Clinton or in the days after the September 11 attacks. I only wish the current leaders of the Senate would take this lesson to heart.

Besides technological changes, another reason there is so little time for members to interact socially and build the relationships needed for bipartisan cooperation is the financial costs of political campaigns today. To run an effective campaign, some candidates for the House need to raise over $1 million, and for the Senate, $10 million. With individual contributions restricted to $2,400 each, members of the House and Senate have to devote an inordinate amount of time to calling potential donors and organizing and attending fundraising events.

I have long been a proponent of campaign finance reform. I worked on the legislation restricting contributions and spending which came after the abuses of the Watergate scandal. I was a member of the Committee for Economic Development, which galvanized business support for the McCain-Feingold law, which banned unlimited contributions of soft money to political parties.

We are now also faced with the prospect of unlimited spending by corporations, following the Citizens United decision of the Supreme Court. The 2012 presidential and congressional election will be the first test of this new influence by corporate money.

Here my recommendation would be for public financing of federal campaigns. As citizens, we should support the use of public resources for a public good—in this case, the process of selecting the best persons to represent us in Congress. Several states and cities have adopted such financing for local campaigns. For example, I understand that here in New York City candidates for public office receive a four-to-one match for small contributions. A similar system for congressional candidates could help ease the relentless chase for dollars, freeing up the time of members of Congress for other business and reducing the influence of large donors and lobbyists. I believe a result would be a more civil discourse in Washington.

Another recommendation for election reform I have is for states to adopt nonpartisan redistricting commissions. I came from a highly competitive district. Only once in my 22 years in Congress did a majority of the voters in my district ever vote for the Democratic presidential nominee, in the LBJ landslide of 1964. What that meant was that as a Democrat, I always had to appeal to a significant number of Republican voters, despite wave elections like 2006 and 2010.

State gerrymandering of districts has made fewer and fewer seats competitive, allowing members during primaries and general elections to appeal to the base of their parties. Nonpartisan redistricting could help produce more moderate representatives who would have to build support among both Democrats and Republicans to win elections and would be more willing to reach across the aisle when they get to Washington.

This brings me to one other question: How can we encourage more of our brightest students to choose careers in politics and public service? Among the activities of my Brademas Center for the Study of Congress at New York University has been a summer congressional internship program. Every summer for the last five years, we have sent down eight undergraduate and graduate students from NYU to work on Capitol Hill in the offices of senators and representatives. We offer stipends to cover the cost of living in Washington for the summer and we organize weekly luncheons and dinners with guest speakers to engage the students. The interns do everything from answering phones to undertaking original policy research. They interact daily with members of Congress and congressional staffers. In September the students present papers based on some aspect of their time on the Hill.

I can report to you that the feedback from students has been overwhelmingly positive. Every year I put the question to them: Would any of you consider returning to Washington to work on Capitol Hill or even to run for Congress? Every one of last year's class indicated that they would seriously become congressional staffers, with even two suggesting they are strongly considering running for elected office. Indeed, several of the alumni from our internship program are now working in the executive and legislative branches.

So I would say the country needs more programs like the one the Brademas Center has organized in order to encourage careers in public service.

I believe that politics is a noble profession. The men and women who serve in Congress—while we may strongly disagree with them on some of the policies they pursue—the majority of them are there because they genuinely believe the work they do will make this country better for their constituents and all Americans. They and their staffers do not live lavish lifestyles, and they often spend 12- to 14-hour days working on the people's business.

But as I have suggested, there are ways to improve civility, which in turn should advance cooperation and consensus on Capitol Hill. As America serves as a model and a light to those countries still struggling for democracy, we owe it to them to show how ideas and policies can be civilly debated and, once adopted by a majority of the democratically elected representatives of the people, respected as the laws of the land.

★

Mickey Edwards

on

Civility in Politics

John Brademas gave a list of things we need. I think the thing we need is more John Brademases. It's true that the times in the past were not always exactly as we might have wished them, but it was a different time. John is a liberal Democrat. I was the national chairman of the American Conservative Union and I was one of the three founders of the Heritage Foundation, and I admire John like crazy. When he put together his Brademas Center, he asked me to be on the advisory board. We have great admiration and respect for each other, because we don't walk around wearing either an R or a D emblazoned into our foreheads.

A couple of observations I want to make:

We seem to believe that we live in a political system in which dominance by two rival political parties is the norm; it's just the way it has always been—the sun comes up in the morning and we have political parties, we have the Republicans and the Democrats to choose between.

Actually, that's not true. The closed party primary system we have now is a relic of the Progressive Movement in the late 1890s, early 1900s. It's not a part of our political constitutional system. Founders James Madison and George Washington both warned against the creation of what we now have as modern political parties. I want to come back to that in a bit.

But just a historical note. There was a time, whether it was Vietnam or other periods like that, when in the streets of the United States there was a great deal of animosity and anger, and there were some people in the Congress who got caught up in that. But even at that time, even in that time when what was happening out in the streets and civil rights and war and other things divided people on great issues, almost every single nominee for the U.S. Supreme Court, whether it was the Douglases or the Frankfurters or the Brandeises, were getting confirmed almost unanimously, bipartisan, both parties. Medicare, Medicaid, most of the great social reform issues were getting passed by overwhelming numbers of people in both political parties. The reason for that was that at that time people understood that when they stepped across the aisle after taking the oath of office—they held up their hands and they were sworn in as members of Congress—they were no longer partisans waging a political battle, but they were members of Congress, the legislative branch of government—the branch of government that has almost all power.

Here's one of the stories that I like to tell. There is a columnist named Dana Milbank for *The Washington Post*, who wrote a column when George W. Bush was president. The president was getting ready to go overseas on a mission. As Milbank put it, the president was getting ready to step out of his role as head of government to function for the next week or so in his other role as head of state.

I was teaching at Princeton at the time. I asked my students, "What jumps out at you about this, that instead of his role as head of government, he's going to act in his role as head of state?"

Of course, the answers were predictable:

- "Well, he's going to be dealing with basing rights."
- "He's going to be dealing with flyovers."
- "He's going to be dealing with trade agreements."

I said, "No. The president is not the head of government. We don't have a head of government. This is not Peru. We have three separate, independent, equal branches of government."

Almost every single major power that ever belonged to any king, dictator, or emperor was left in the hands of the people through their representatives—war power, spending power, taxing power, program creations—all of them in Congress. That's why this issue of being able to have legislative bodies that can work together instead of just brawling with each other is fundamental to our ability to keep our society going.

When Benjamin Franklin was asked—everybody thinks this is apocryphal, but it's not—"What kind of government have you given us?" when they came out of Constitution Hall, he said, "A republic, madam, if you can keep it."

I wrote a column once that said that that was apocryphal, and the expert on Benjamin Franklin, Walter Isaacson, who is my boss, said, "No. It happened. Here's when and here's where," and so forth.

Franklin said, "A republic, if you can keep it."

When Abraham Lincoln was speaking at Gettysburg and he was describing why we were in a civil war, he said, "It's a test of whether or not a nation so conceived could long endure."

Whether or not it could long endure is whether or not we continue to see ourselves primarily as Americans in a common nation with a common cause and common goals or as separate rival clubs unable to talk to each other.

John Brademas used the word "consensus." Consensus is not possible. There are 300 million of us, with different backgrounds, different experiences. The problem is, when consensus is not possible, compromise becomes indispensable. You have to be able to compromise. When we have drawn the lines based on our party identities, compromise becomes impossible.

I should throw in here—this is a little bit of a plug—a mention of my article in *The Atlantic* in the July-August 2011 issue. I didn't write the title; I just wrote the article. The editors of *The Atlantic* wrote the title, but I like it. It's "How to Turn Republicans and Democrats into Americans." That's something worth considering.

John Brademas discussed some of the problems. I'll just mention a couple of others.

When John and I were there, part of the reason we were able to compromise and get along and be friends had to do with who we are, but some of it was that that was a different time. It was a different environment. It was before Glenn Beck. It was before Rush Limbaugh. It was before Keith Olbermann. It was before Roger Ailes. It was when people who were in the media business, television and radio, thought that they had higher obligations than simply pursuing the making of money, whatever that took.

There was an article, I think it was in the *The New York Times*, quoting Lawrence O'Donnell, who now has a primetime show, in which he talked about how he is having to readjust his thinking in order to fit the model that they have on MSNBC, the model being that it has to be nasty; it has to be confrontational.

I once said—this is not very nice, and I'm trying to give you the impression that I'm a civil guy—I suggested once that we should take Rush Limbaugh and Keith Olbermann and drop them off the same bridge at the same time. That's probably not the best approach.

So part of it is the role that the media has played. Part of it is the way that the Congress has adjusted its schedule so that members are no longer there and able to get to know each other, as John and I got to know each other. Part of it is the raising of money, which takes part of the time that you would use to get to know each other. In fact, getting money often requires you to be in line with somebody who has a very strong agenda that they want to pursue and which will brook no disagreement.

I agree completely with John about redistricting. What we have now is a war between two private clubs. The Republicans and Democrats are not in the Constitution. They are not part of our system. They are two private clubs to which we have surrendered the power to govern elections. Let me give you a couple of examples.

Congressional district lines are drawn by whichever party controls the majority in a state legislature. I don't know how many of you have been to Oklahoma. It's a big state. Every bit of New England fits inside of Oklahoma. I had a congressional district that was in the middle of the state, completely urban. Oklahoma City's population is the same size as Boston's. I'm a city dude. I really am. I won a district that had been held by Democrats since 1928. My district was 75 percent Democrat. I won it, and I won it again. And it just drove the Democrats crazy. They controlled our state legislature at that time by a margin of about nine to one, and so they redrew the congressional district lines, taking me from the center of the state all the way up to Kansas, which is a long way, and then halfway over to Arkansas. A big, upside-down L is the way they gerrymandered my district. They did this to put every Republican they could find in Oklahoma into my district and take them all out of the other districts so they would be safer for Democrats.

For years, I kept saying, "Look what they did to me. Poor me." But they didn't do it to me at all. There is a provision in the Constitution that everybody kind of overlooks that says that every single senator and representative has to be an inhabitant of the state from which they are elected. The purpose is that this powerful group that makes all the laws is going to be made up of people who are your neighbors, that your member of the Senate or of the House knows you, knows your problems, knows your concerns. That's self-rule. That's how we became citizens, not subjects. We would be selected by our neighbors.

You know what? Instead of a district like Boston, I had a district that was full of wheat farmers and cattle ranchers and wonderful people. I knew them and I loved them, and I knew nothing about agricultural issues. I didn't care about agricultural issues. I didn't want to know anything about agricultural issues. They were no longer represented by somebody who could speak for them adequately, accurately, and smartly in Congress. That was because we allow the political parties to decide what our congressional district lines are going to be like.

So I also am in favor of nonpartisan redistricting commissions. Thirteen states now have something like that, in one form or another. But there are others.

The state of Delaware has about a million people. In the primaries in the midterms last time, if you had taken a poll in the state of Delaware, an overwhelming majority would have supported Mike Castle for his seat in the U.S. Senate. Instead, he had to go through a party primary in which, out of the 1 million people in Delaware, only 30,000 voted for a woman named Christine O'Donnell, and Mike Castle could no longer be on the ballot in November.

In Utah, which has 3 million people, 3,500 went to a convention and chose Mike Lee instead of Senator Robert Bennett, who was very popular in the state, for a Senate seat.

The city and state governments have surrendered control over the election process to two private clubs.

A long time ago, the state of Louisiana, where you don't often look for progressive movement, said, "We're not going to do that. We're going to have primaries that are open to everybody. Everybody who wants to run for governor, Congress, or whatever is on the same ballot, and everybody who wants to vote in that race can vote in that same race."

Washington State adopted that in 2006. California adopted it in the last midterm elections, in 2010.

The idea of taking away from parties the right to tell us who can be on the ballot in November, who we can choose between, is an absolutely essential reform to putting the people back in control and getting away from this system that always elects more and more partisan zealots, because you have to go through this narrow party primary fight.

The third thing is when I took the oath of office, stepped across this magic line, and instead of a Republican candidate, I became a member of the lawmaking branch of the U.S. government. I was in a group of fairly well-known people. I was the least known among them. Al Gore was in that class, Dick Gephardt, Dan Quayle. We had a good group of people. We were all there together. We were all equal. We were all members of the new class and members of Congress.

That lasted about 30 seconds. Then we divided into two rival clubs to decide who would be speaker, what the rules would be, how many people could serve on what committee. And it has continued on that basis. You really don't have a U.S. House of Representatives. You have two rival U.S. Houses of Representatives occupying the same space.

I was on the very illustriously named Committee on Committees. Wait a minute. I'll show off more: I was on the Executive Committee of the Committee on Committees. What we did was, we chose who got to serve on what committee. How did the leadership do that? I was chairman of the Republican Policy Committee. How did the leadership do that? You would go and you would say, "If you want a seat on Ways and Means, here are the issues that are fundamental to our party position. You can get that seat if you promise to be true to the party position."

Why do we let party leaders, club leaders, decide who is going to serve on what committees? If you decided you were going to get together to do something for the Carnegie Council, you would sit and have a conversation, and I guarantee you, you wouldn't decide, "Okay, Republicans, sit over there; Democrats, sit over there." You wouldn't do that in most places where we decide things important in this country. But we allow that to happen in Congress.

Why do we let party leaders do that? There are so many other ways—strictly by seniority, regardless of party, by a drawing. There are lots of ways to choose who serves on what committee, all of them elected by the same number of people.

I'll pick up on something John Brademas said that was accurate. As the chairman of his subcommittee, as he said, he did not need to ask the minority ranking member who he wanted to have testify. John is the kind of person that *did* ask him. Some chairmen don't ask them. Why do we allow whoever happens to be the most senior member of a committee to decide who gets to testify, who we'll listen to, what advice we'll get? I'm advocating strongly that we break that.

After I left Congress, I taught at Harvard for 11 years and then I taught at Princeton. Now I'm a vice president of the Aspen Institute. I run a program that brings together—I'm the entire admissions committee; I have a great job—every year 12 Democrats and 12 Republicans from throughout the United States who hold public office, elective office, and bring them together into a fellowship. One now is in the Senate, two are governors, five are in the U.S. House, the attorneys general of a lot of our different states, lieutenant governors of a lot of our states, and the mayors of Atlanta, Charlotte, San Antonio, and Baltimore are all part of my program.

What we do is—this is an Aspen Institute thing—we don't talk about Iraq and we don't talk about health care; we talk about Plato, Aristotle, Confucius, Locke, Amartya Sen, and Virginia

Woolf. We talk about principles and ideas, about what binds us together as believers in democracy, not as members of club A or club B. Then we also take them to China, India, Egypt, and Israel to meet with government leaders and really understand the issues that are arising in those areas. It's about a new kind of politics. It's a politics that is not based in party.

It's one of the great, amazing things to me. I have chosen all of these people. The very first one we ever chose, seven years ago, was Gabby Giffords. There will be 24 people sitting around a table having conversations about all of these ideas. I can't remember who is a Republican and who is a Democrat. When you strip away the party loyalty and talk about values, principles, and ideals, they are all the same. They are all just Americans.

So that's one of the changes we need to make to get to the kind of a system that was personified by people like John Brademas.

★

Charles Osgood

on

Civility in the Media

I must begin with a disclaimer. I do not hold myself to be an expert on the subject of civility in the media, nor am I holier than thou or more civil than thou or than my colleagues and competitors in radio and television. I sit in judgment on no one. But I do have some thoughts on the subject that I'm happy to pass on.

The subject itself may be an oxymoron or, at the very least, a paradox. You may be familiar with the observation that military justice is to justice what military music is to music. As someone whose military career consisted of three years as a member of the United States Army Band, I know about that. I also recognize the inherent paradox of having a guy who does what I do for a living talk about civility at all.

What we try to create on Sunday mornings is, at best, the illusion of civility. We do try to hold the yelling and screaming down to an absolute minimum on the *Sunday Morning* set. But those of you who watch the broadcast may have noticed that I have a little IFB [Interrupted Feedback] in my ear. Its purpose is to keep me in touch with the control room to tell me things that they feel I must know and also to be aware of what is going on in the control room.

I can hear what's being said in the control room, and I can assure you, there is a certain amount of yelling and screaming going on. It's inevitable. It just goes with the territory.

We had a cardiac specialist appearing as a guest once. It was not on *Sunday Morning*, but it was on a morning news broadcast that I was involved with. The president of the United States was traveling, and things were being shifted around, such that this person who was to be a guest was moved back later in the broadcast because the plane was late with the president arriving in Moscow.

When it was over, the producer went up to the doctor and said, "I'm terribly sorry for having done this to you, but you can see the kinds of problems we were having, so we had to put you on at the end of the program."

She said, "All you people are going to die. I have never seen anything like that in my life."

The point that she wanted to make was that strife and stress would take a terrible toll on a person, not only mentally, but as far as circulation and well-being is concerned.

It does go with the territory in television. You can kind of get used to it, but it takes somebody from the outside to notice it and point it out, as this woman did.

Any of you who have ever met Shad Northshield or know him in any way, he was the founding producer of *Sunday Morning* and a man of tremendous sensitivity—most of the time. Or perhaps you have met Bill Leonard, the president of CBS News at the time, who commissioned *Sunday Morning*, or the incomparable host for the first 16 years of *Sunday Morning*, Charles Kuralt, my friend and my mentor.

What they produced may have been inspiring, but what Thomas Edison said about inspiration and perspiration applies here. You do not want to be there when the sausage is made, let's put it that way. But I admired all of them immensely, and I don't want to forget what they taught me over the years about what it is that we're trying to do on *Sunday Morning*.

Charles was known for his *On the Road* series. He did not like to attend news conferences and be one of a pack of newsmen standing behind a rope and shouting out questions to somebody who was going to be on the evening news that night. He did not like that sort of encounter. He liked to be alone. He liked to spend time with people that he admired, not necessarily people who were making news in the view of somebody else, but people that he wanted to become engaged with and find out more about.

Charles did get some criticism for this. He told me that people had chewed him out for this, saying that it's not appropriate for us news reporters to admire their subjects. We're supposed to investigate them, he was told, and find out what ugly secrets they are trying to hide. He never thought that a good story would be a better one if you kept your fangs bared and your claws unsheathed and were able to succeed in bringing somebody down in your report, leaving them in a pool of blood.

One of the unfortunate legacies of Watergate is that it bred a whole generation of journalists who got into the business because they wanted to demonize; they wanted to bring somebody down; they wanted to tear the masks off the bad guys. There are plenty of bad guys, and I'm glad there are broadcasts, like our *60 Minutes*, that tell people what they need to know. We do that, too, on *Sunday Morning* in our own way. We think it is possible to educate, to inform, and to inspire an audience. I always watch *60 Minutes*, and I'm proud of what my colleagues there do. I always learn something from it that I didn't know before, and that is useful and constructive.

I always learn from *Sunday Morning*, too. It's one of the tremendous things about being in this business, that you get to meet fantastic people that in the ordinary course of events, that if you were doing something else for a living, you would never get to meet.

I'm going soon to the Franklin Institute in Philadelphia, where they give out the Franklin Institute Awards. I did the emceeing of that ceremony last year, and I got to have lunch with Bill Gates, who was one of the awardees for the work that he has done. I'm doing it again this year. Because some of the winners are involved in genetic work, I looked back in my own files to see what I knew about the subject of DNA and genetics, and whom I learned it from. I learned it from James Watson at Cold Spring Harbor and from Francis Crick, at the Salk Institute, where he was living at the time. This was on some anniversary—maybe it was the 25th anniversary—of their discovery of the double helix and how DNA works. And there they were, the two of them. I looked with dismay at a much younger me and a much younger Watson and Crick. Francis Crick has died in the meantime.

They talked about what fun it was to be working on this particular problem, and how the only thing that bothered them was that it seemed so simple once it was done. It all seemed perfectly obvious—of course the magic number was 2. They identified the proteins that made up the base pairs that not only told you what was in there, but how it works to make reproduction possible for all living creatures. A fantastic breakthrough, and I got to hear it from those guys themselves. That's a tremendous privilege. When Richard Salant, longtime president of CBS News, was asked once by a group of children, "What do you like most about being the president of CBS News?" He said, "You probably don't think learning is very enjoyable, but the most enjoyable thing about working at CBS News is that you learn something every day."

However, there are circumstances under which you cannot learn. Basically, if you are involved in conversation with somebody and you do not listen, then you will learn nothing. If what you are doing in an interview is trying to think of the next question that you are going to ask, then you will only know that your subject was finished with his talk when he stops talking, and then you can go ahead with the question that you were thinking of asking. But there's no dialogue there and there's no opportunity for you to learn.

There is an old poem that I heard for the first time from Ted Turner, on his boat the year that he won the America's Cup. You wonder, what does the captain of a racing sailboat in the America's Cup do? He would yell at people. He was not shy about doing that himself. But he said, "Mainly I have to listen."

Did you ever hear this poem?

A wise old bird sat in an oak.
The more he saw, the less he spoke.
The less he spoke, the more he heard.
Why aren't we like that wise old bird?

When anybody asks me, "What's the secret of doing an interview?" I have to tell them, listen. Don't just listen for the words and their cognitive, literal meanings, but listen for the connotations. You will learn something if you do that, and the next question will come to you growing out of what you have just learned.

If you are hell-bent on trying to find out the flaw in what somebody is saying so that you can pounce and make them yell or cry. If they cry, that's perfect; that's really what you want them to do, or to just break down and say, "Oh, you're right. I was wrong all along." That doesn't happen very much, let me tell you.

People in television who put themselves and their opinions front and center—that is, wait for the opportunity to say what you think, not try to find out what the other person thinks, and who believe that what the public wants is not light, but heat; the more heat, the better—the more incivility there is going to be and the less we're all going to learn from watching such a person on television.

Maybe it's generational. I'm 78 now. I think we were better off when politeness counted in politics and just in life in general.

On your report card, when I was a kid, at our Lady of Lourdes grammar school in Baltimore, Maryland, there was one category called "Deportment." Remember that? Nobody grades you on deportment at all anymore. It's a good thing they don't, given what the deportment is. In those days, men tipped their hats to women, removed their hats in an elevator, offered their seats on a bus or a train, held the door, ladies first. Nowadays, some women feel insulted if you hold the door for them. I think that's a shame. Call me old-fashioned.

It seems to me that we use coarser language now. Remember Cole Porter's lyrics—people "who once knew better words now only use four-letter words writing prose... Anything goes." That has only gotten worse since Cole Porter was writing his songs.

In speech, in dress, in the way we deal with people, there is not as much refinement as there once was. Maybe it's an effort to be more democratic. For years and years and years, Walter Cronkite and then Dan Rather opened the *Evening News* by saying, "Good evening." From the day that Katie Couric sat in that chair, the opening greeting was, "Hi." That's what people really say. That's the language that people use these days. It's picking up the language of the street so that the people who are watching will relate to you more; they will identify with you better.

I live across the street from Carnegie Hall. It's great living over there, because you can look out the window and say, "The concert starts in five minutes. Maybe we should mosey on over there."

People are going to hear great music played by great artists, who are dressed in formal attire, because the occasion seems to call for that, in respect to the great music, and about half the people in the Hall look as if they're dressed to go fishing. That's too bad.

I wear a tie and a jacket on television. I don't always wear a tie and a jacket, but I do when I'm going to Carnegie Hall. I do when I'm going out for the evening and going to be among people. You take pleasure in dressing to fit the occasion. But we're not like that anymore. People who are running for president hardly ever wear a tie. You take the tie off and maybe you hold the jacket over your shoulder. You want to show that you're a man of the people. In television we do much the same thing.

I am not somebody who uses my name a lot. I use it at the beginning of the broadcast and again at the end, an hour and a half later, and nowhere in between. Like my longtime friend and amazing anchorman Walter Cronkite, I don't believe in use of the first-person singular in your reporting.

E.B. White said in *The Elements of Style*, a re-write of a book that had been done by his teacher at Cornell, "For good writing, keep yourself in the background." That also applies to telling a good news story, unless what you are trying to do is call attention to yourself.

On the sign for *Sunday Morning*, it says it's *CBS Sunday Morning*. It's not *Sunday Morning* with me. It's just the broadcast. I'm not the first person to do it and I'm not going to be the last. It is a tradition, however, that the next person has to be named Charles. I think it must save the company money somehow on the IDs.

I used to do the Sunday night news, a 15-minute broadcast. Then I would get up and do the radio the next morning. The end piece on the broadcast was something that they called *The Osgood File*. One of *The Osgood File* things that we did was a piece on the anniversary of the Senate Foreign Relations Committee hearings on Vietnam—terribly important, so important to CBS that we lost Fred Friendly over it. He wanted us to carry those hearings, and the television people said, "No. We have people waiting to see *The Guiding Light*," and whatever else was going to be on in the afternoon. It was commercial time, so it was important that we stick to the program schedule.

My producer, Jim Ganzer, talked with Senator Fulbright, who was by that time retired, living back in Arkansas, but he had come back to Washington for the occasion. He recalled, "Those were very important hearings, because America learned things that they didn't know. I think the president learned things that he didn't know."

He said the president had called him at one time and said, "Bill, where are you getting this stuff that you're saying in your columns?"

What Fulbright said was, "I didn't make it up. I got it from Walter Lippmann."

Lyndon Johnson said, "Tell you what. Next time you need a dam in Arkansas, you call Walter Lippmann."

Senator Fulbright told my producer Jim, "We had wonderful people testifying. We had Charles Osgood down here. He testified at those hearings."

Jim said, "He did?" He couldn't imagine how that could be.

He said, "Oh, yes. He's the man when it comes to disarmament and negotiations and all that kind of thing."

He was talking about Professor Charles E. Osgood, who taught for many years at the University of Illinois at Champaign-Urbana and whose specialty was psychosemantics. He was a psychologist. He studied the connotative meaning of words and learned how to measure it. From that, he got into disarmament and something called GRIT that he had introduced, the concept of "gradual reductions in terror" by coming to agreements on things that you could agree on, by using words that could be accepted by both sides.

Then it happened that I went to Champaign-Urbana and he called me. He said he had always wanted to meet me because he figured we must be related. I knew that that wasn't true, because my last name is Wood. Osgood is my middle name. It was my father's middle name and it was my grandfather's middle name. He said, "I think we must be related, because there's only one Osgood family that came over," and he told me all about them. It was fascinating stuff.

One of the Osgoods, Samuel Osgood, was a dear friend of George Washington. When George Washington was the president of the United States and the capital of the United States was New York City—there was no White House—the president lived with his friend Samuel Adams right here in Manhattan. Samuel Adams became the first postmaster general of the United States.

Anyway, the fact was that he was somebody that Senator Fulbright and others could remember years later because he had been in the business of looking at words and trying to use the right words that would not turn somebody off, words where an agreement could be made step by step, until you could achieve some progress, as we did in disarmament with the Soviet Union.

As far as I'm concerned, he was one of the important people that I got to meet. I said, "What made you want to call me?"

He said, "Well, I'm sick and tired of people asking me if I'm the one who writes those silly poems on the radio."

He died about 12 years ago. He was another fellow I was glad I had a chance to meet. I learned something from him.

There was a time when I was in the Army Band that I got to meet a few politicians. The Army Band was known as "Pershing's Own." The band had traveled with Eisenhower during World War II, so it was "Eisenhower's Own" at that time. Eisenhower was president of the United States at the time I'm talking about.

When I was in the Army Band, I wrote the lyrics to the trio section of a stately march called "Gallant Men" by John Cacavas. We lived off-post and Cacavas was my roommate. He was an arranger and composer.

Senator Everett McKinley Dirksen, Republican of Illinois, would later make a hit recording of that song, reading my lyrics. I'm sure many of you will remember minority leader or majority leader of the Senate, Everett Dirksen (depending on which party was in control), and his opposite number for the Democrats was a fellow by the name of Lyndon

Johnson, Democrat of Texas, who would later become president.

Those two men were both politically astute. They disagreed with one another about almost everything. But they did have respect for one another and were able to work with one another to get things done for the people. At the end of almost every day, they would meet and have a drink together.

Can you imagine that today? It's almost unthinkable—congressional leaders of both parties having a drink and coming to know and respect each other, even though they disagreed so much. Isn't it sad that such a thing seems out of the question now? And what a price we pay.

Television is responsible for this, too—the person who has the sharpest sound bite as an answer in an interview, he'll make it on the air. Somebody who may have a very well-reasoned answer to the question that makes allowances for why people might feel one way and other people might feel another— that won't make it because it takes 18 seconds, and that's way too much time to waste of valuable television time.

You have to avoid what Carl Sandburg called the "proud words." Maybe some of my friends and colleagues in television never read what Carl Sandburg said about those: "Look out how you use proud words. When you let proud words go, it is not easy to call them back. They wear long, hard boots. They walk off proud. They can't hear a thing."

Those are the thoughts that I have on the subject of civility and its value in the media or in anything else.

★

Robert L. Dilenschneider

Founder and Principal
The Dilenschneider Group, Inc.

It is a great honor to be given the opportunity to end such a collection of wisdom as is this book with a closing commentary. Likewise is it an Aristotelian challenge to substantively add to the thinking already presented by its contributors.

It is, however, a distinct advantage to write the closing chapter, as from here an author has a unique perspective of common threads and themes present in the writings.

One clear theme is this: Civility is a responsibility that comes with the privilege of citizenship. Unfortunately, the passions and politics of recent years have caused the separation of the two, and this has contributed to our current crisis of civic incivility.

As Philip Howard has shared with us, the concept of civility goes back to the origins of communal life, and describes the "norms and manners required to live in a city or crowded place" as well as a "respect for the common good."

Indeed, the idea is rooted in the very belief in the concept of "Citizen Romani"—that being a citizen of ancient Rome was a special and unique honor, giving its bearer the right to engage in public discourse and to influence public laws through the privilege of voting. Roman citizenship was not doled out to any and all who desired it. Families and individuals had to demonstrate an active history, or at least an active interest, in the stability and betterment of Roman society in order to participate as citizens.

This belief in the honor which Roman citizenship conferred to a person was so bedrock that it often stood in rigid defense of even the most disliked voices. It was St. Paul's declaration to a Roman centurion about to scourge him—"Civis Romanus sum" ("I am a Roman citizen")—that stayed the lash and required that he be taken to Rome for a trial by his fellow-citizen peers, as was the right of a citizen.

If citizenship bestowed upon St. Paul the right to be heard, even to spread sedition (with civility) until impeded by a trial by fellow Romans—how far the

honor of citizenship has fallen that Americans cannot engage in civil debate over even trifling subjects
of far less importance than life or death?

As noted in this book, mid-19th century British
jurist Lord Moulton clearly found that "between can
do and may do ought to exist the whole realm which
recognizes the sway of duty, fairness, sympathy,
taste, and all the other things that make life beautiful and society possible." In other words, not all
things that should be can be codified in law or en-
forced by legal means.

His words speak to another aspect of civility,
which has not been honored enough in the public
square of late: that is a due respect for the institutions and practices that have caused our society to be
uniquely great.

My friend Henry Kaufman notes that financial
markets and those who participate in them rely on
"normal" behaviors—behaviors based on well established and proven norms of traditions and ethics.
He is right that "breathtaking change erodes respect
for old ways," and has cited how it was the creation
and rise of the precarious derivatives market that led
his own beloved Salomon Brothers to eschew its
foundation of stability and eventually stumble and
fall.

Would this have happened if a proper respect (a
proper civility) had been afforded the hard lessons
learned by those who had brought Salomon Broth-

ers to the heights from which it crashed? Probably not. The company's management would have been guided by a respect for solid practices that had gone before; instead, such practices were viewed as "ancient history" with no relevance to the "unique challenges" of the day.

Henry reminds us—and all who will someday face an "unprecedented crisis" in their day—of Mark Twain's wise counsel that "History may not repeat itself, but it does rhyme." A civility and respect toward that which has gone before can usually offer valuable guidance in most crisis situations, whether of divine or human origin.

All too often problems are of our own making, and in those cases we would do well to remember the sage words of CBS's Charles Osgood, who reminds us there are only a few circumstances under which we cannot learn, and one of them is "If you do not listen, then you will learn nothing."

That thought was offered for the benefit of budding journalists, but there are few engaged in civic debate for whom it does not hold good advice. Listening is a practice that has, unfortunately, fallen far too out of favor. As nature abhors a vacuum, so, too, do many people abhor the absence of their own voices. This can block all incoming communication in favor of the royal "I" and an exclusive focus on one's own point of view.

At such times we would do well to remember the words of Carl Sandburg concerning what the poet called "proud words."

"Look out how you use proud words," Sandburg admonished. "When you let proud words go, it is not easy to call them back. They wear long, hard boots. They walk off proud. They can't hear a thing."

With so many people of good heart and mind focusing on our crisis of incivility in public life, however, it is my hope and belief (as it is several of the book's contributors) that within the next decade we will begin to see a change for the positive.

It is the great strength of our nation that periods of raucous discourse, though painful to watch, lead to a pause in the battle and the emergence of a more civil discourse.

Let it begin with careful consideration of the wisdom in this book, which can lead our country to a reconnection between its citizenry and a time in which civility once again rules the day.

BIOGRAPHIES

(in alphabetical order)

JOHN BRADEMAS represented Indiana's 3rd District in the U.S. House of Representatives from 1959–1981. During his tenure, Dr. Brademas served on the Congressional Committee on Education and Labor, Committee on House Administration, and the Joint Committee on the Library of Congress.

Following a distinguished career in Congress, from 1981–1992 Dr. Brademas served as President of New York University.

Dr. Brademas served as Chairman of the President's Committee on the Arts and the Humanities, the National Endowment for Democracy, and the Board of the Federal Reserve Bank of New York. Currently, he is president of the King Juan Carlos I of Spain Center of New York University Foundation, a Fellow of the American Academy of Arts and Sciences and member of the National Academy of Education, The Academy of Athens, European Academy of Science and Arts, and National Academy of Education of Argentina. In 2004 the New York State Legislature elected him to the New York State Board of Regents.

After graduating magna cum laude from Harvard University, Dr. Brademas won a Rhodes scholarship and earned his Ph.D. at Brasenose College, University of Oxford. He has been awarded honorary degrees by 52 colleges and universities, most recently in 2003 from the University of Oxford. Among numerous other honors, he has received the Hubert H. Humphrey Award of the American Political Science Association for outstanding public service by a political scientist.

ROBERT L. DILENSCHNEIDER is Founder and Principal of The Dilenschneider Group, a New York–based corporate communications firm. Prior to founding The Dilenschneider Group in 1991, Mr. Dilenschneider served as president and Chief Executive Officer of Hill & Knowlton from 1986 to 1991. He has counseled hundreds of clients, among them major corporations, professional groups, trade associations and educational institutions.

Mr. Dilenschneider has authored eight books— including the best-selling *Power and Influence*, *A Briefing for Leaders*, *On Power*, *The Critical 14 Years of Your Professional Life*, *Moses: C.E.O,* and *The*

Critical 2nd Phase of your Professional Life. Most recently, he published *The AMA Handbook of Public Relations.* He has lectured before scores of professional organizations and colleges, including the University of Notre Dame, Ohio State University, New York University and The Harvard Business School, and has served on numerous corporate boards.

Mr. Dilenschneider started his career in public relations in 1967. He received a M.A. in journalism from Ohio State University and a B.A. from the University of Notre Dame.

MICKEY EDWARDS served for eight terms as a member of the U.S. House of Representatives from Oklahoma's 5th Congressional District. During his Congressional career, he was a member of the Appropriations and Budget Committees and the ranking member of the Subcommittee on Foreign Operations, and was a senior member of the House Republican leadership. Mr. Edwards was the director of the congressional policy task force that advised Ronald Reagan's 1980 presidential campaign. He was one of the three founding trustees of the Heritage Foundation and national chairman of the American Conservative Union, and served for five years as chairman of the annual Conservative Political Action Conference.

After 16 years in Congress, Mr. Edwards taught at Harvard's John F. Kennedy School of Government for 11 years. He was a visiting lecturer at Harvard Law School and a visiting professor at Georgetown University. He was also an advisor to the State Department under Secretary of State Colin Powell. Currently, Mr. Edwards is a lecturer at Princeton's Woodrow Wilson School of Public and International Affairs and directs a political leadership program for the Aspen Institute.

Mr. Edwards serves on the Board of Directors of The Constitution Project and has chaired task forces for the Brookings Institution and the Council on Foreign Relations. He has been a regular political commentator on National Public Radio's "All Things Considered" and author of a weekly political column appearing in the *Chicago Tribune, Los Angeles Times, Boston Herald* and other major newspapers.

STEVE FORBES is President and Chief Executive Officer of Forbes and Editor-in-Chief of *Forbes* magazine. He is also Chairman of the company's American Heritage division, publisher of *American Heritage* magazine and two quarterlies, *American Legacy* and *American Heritage of Invention & Technology*.

In 1985, President Ronald Reagan named Mr. Forbes Chairman of the bi-partisan Board for International Broadcasting (BIB). In this position, he oversaw the operation of Radio Free Europe and Radio Liberty. Mr. Forbes was reappointed to his post by President George H. W. Bush and served until 1993. In both 1996 and 2000, Mr. Forbes campaigned for the Republican Presidential nomination. Key to his platform were a flat tax, medical savings accounts, a new Social Security system for working Americans, parental choice of schools for their children, term limits, and a strong national defense.

Mr. Forbes is the author of *A New Birth of Freedom* (Regnery, 1999), a book of bold ideas for the new millennium. He received a B.A. in history from Princeton University in 1970 and holds honorary degrees from Lycoming College, Jacksonville University, Heidelberg College, Iona College, Kean College, New York Institute of Technology, Lock Haven University, Westminster College, Francisco Marroquin University (Guatemala), Sacred Heart University, Centenary College, Pepperdine University, Lynn University, Lehigh University, New Hampshire College, Siena College, Universidad Espiritu Santo (Ecuador), Lincoln College, New Bulgarian University, Spring Arbor University, Seton Hall University, Raritan Valley Community College and Caldwell College.

THE REV. THEODORE MARTIN HESBURGH is President Emeritus of the University of Notre Dame. He is known internationally for his work promoting justice and peace.

Rev. Hesburgh served as Notre Dame's President for 35 years, the longest presidential tenure at the University to date. He has served on 16 presidential commissions, and is currently the co-chair of the United States Institute of Peace's National Campaign for Peacemaking.

In 1967, he led an academic movement that issued the so-called "Land O'Lakes" statement, insisting upon "true autonomy and academic freedom in the face of authority of whatever kind, lay or clerical." He was among the founders of People for the American Way and served on the Knight Commission on Intercollegiate Athletics. Rev. Hesburgh remains an influential figure in U.S. politics and the Catholic Church. He is an advocate for the Genocide Intervention Network and an ardent supporter of interfaith dialogue.

Rev. Hesburgh studied at The Holy Cross seminary at Notre Dame until being relocated to the Gregorian University in Rome, where he earned a bachelor's degree in philosophy. He later graduated from The Catholic University of America with a Doctorate in Sacred Theology. Rev. Hesburgh was the recipient of the Presidential Medal of Freedom in 1964, and in 2000 he was the first person from higher education to be awarded the Congressional Gold Medal.

PHILIP K. HOWARD is vice-chairman of Covington and Burling, LLP, and the founder of Common Good. He has advised national political leaders on legal and regulatory reform since the 1990s and has authored numerous books, including *Life Without Lawyers*, as well as the bestsellers *The Death of Common Sense* and *The Collapse of the Common Good*. He also wrote the introduction to Vice President Al Gore's book, *Common Sense Government*.

Mr. Howard contributes to the *Wall Street Journal, The Washington Post*, and *The New York Times*, and has appeared on *The Daily Show* with Jon Stewart, *Oprah, Today, Good Morning America, Charlie Rose, PBS NewsHour* with Jim Lehrer, *20/20* and *Nightline*, among other numerous programs.

In 2002, Mr. Howard founded Common Good, a national bipartisan coalition organized to restore common sense to American public life. With the cooperation of a number of nonprofit organizations, Mr. Howard recently founded NewTalk.org, an online forum of thought leaders.

Mr. Howard has long been a civic leader in New York. He is chair of the committee that installed the "Tribute in Light" Memorial, which honors the victims of the September 11th terrorist attacks. He is also chair-emeritus of the Municipal Art Society of New York.

HENRY KAUFMAN is president and founder of Henry Kaufman & Company Inc., a consulting firm established in April 1988 specializing in investment management and economic and financial consulting.

Before founding Henry Kaufman & Company, Dr. Kaufman for 26 years worked at Salomon Brothers Inc., where he was a managing director, a member of the executive committee, and head of the firm's four research departments. Before joining Salomon Brothers, Dr. Kaufman served as an economist at the Federal Reserve Bank of New York.

Dr. Kaufman is the author of *The Road to Financial Reformation: Warnings, Consequences, Reforms* (2009). Dr. Kaufman received a B.A. in economics from New York University, M.S. in finance from Columbia University, and a Ph.D. from the New York University's Stern School of Business.

CHARLES OSGOOD is a radio and television commentator and author, anchoring CBS News *Sunday Morning* and *The Osgood File*. He writes a bi-weekly syndicated newspaper column, and is the author of six books, most recently *Defending Baltimore Against Enemy Attack* in 2004.

In 1990, Mr. Osgood was inducted into the National Association of Broadcasters Hall of Fame, and into the Broadcasting and Cable Hall of Fame in 2000. In 2005, Mr. Osgood received the Walter

Cronkite Excellence in Journalism Award from Arizona State University. He was the recipient of the 2005 Paul White Award, presented by the Radio-Television News Directors Association, for lifetime contribution to electronic journalism. In 2008, Mr. Osgood was recognized with the National Association of Broadcasters Distinguished Service Award.

Mr. Osgood graduated from Fordham University in 1954 with a B.S degree with a major in economics. Mr. Osgood served in the U.S. Army from 1955–1959, where he was as a member of The United States Army Band.

JOEL H. ROSENTHAL is President of the Carnegie Council for Ethics in International Affairs. Founded in 1914 to promote the principles of pluralism and peace, the Council is one of Andrew Carnegie's original peace endowments.

Dr. Rosenthal is editor-in-chief of *Ethics & International Affairs* and the author of *Righteous Realists*. He has co-edited several collections of articles and written numerous articles of his own including "Ethics" in Bruce W. Jentleson, et al.'s *Encyclopedia of U.S. Foreign Relations*. He is currently working on *How Moral Can We Get? Essays on the Moral Nation*.

Dr. Rosenthal received his Ph.D. from Yale University and B.A. from Harvard University. He serves as Senior Fellow of the Stockdale Center at the U.S. Naval Academy and as an adjunct professor at New

York University. He is Chairman of the Bard College Globalization and International Affairs Program in New York City, a committee member of Review of Ethics and International Affairs at Shanghai International Studies University, and an Honorary Professor of History at the University of Copenhagen.

Please visit **www.Dilenschneider.com**
to find more books, reports, and white papers
on topics like this one.

Made in the USA
Charleston, SC
15 October 2011